KARY OBERBRUNNER

THE DEEPER PATH

A SIMPLE METHOD
FOR FINDING CLARITY,
MASTERING LIFE,
AND DOING
YOUR PURPOSE
EVERY DAY

AUTHOR
ACADEMY elite

Also by Kary Oberbrunner

ELIXIR PROJECT
DAY JOB TO DREAM JOB
YOUR SECRET NAME
THE FINE LINE
CALLED
THE JOURNEY TOWARDS RELEVANCE

Published by Author Academy Elite
P.O. Box 43, Powell, OH 43065
www.AuthorAcademyElite.com

Library of Congress Cataloging 2018939597

Softcover: 978-1-64085-268-6
Hardcover: 978-1-64085-269-3
Audiobook: 978-1-64085-270-9

Available in hardcover, softcover, e-book, and audiobook

All Scripture quotations, unless otherwise indicated, are taken from the Holy Bible, *New International Version*®, *NIV*®. Copyright © 1973, 1978, 1984 by Biblica, Inc.™ Used by permission of Zondervan. All rights reserved worldwide.

Scripture quotations marked TNIV are taken from the Holy Bible, *Today's New International Version*™. *TNIV*®. Copyright © 2001, 2005 by Biblica, Inc.™ Used by permission of Zondervan. All rights reserved worldwide.

Scripture quotations marked NASB are taken from the *New American Standard Bible*®, Copyright © 1960, 1962, 1963, 1968, 1971, 1972, 1973, 1975, 1977, 1995 by The Lockman Foundation. Used by permission.

To protect the privacy of those who have shared their stories with the author, some details and names have been changed. Any internet addresses (websites, blogs, etc.) and telephone numbers printed in this book are offered as a resource. They are not intended in any way to be or imply an endorsement by Author Academy Elite, nor does Author Academy Elite vouch for the content of these sites and numbers for the life of this book.

CONTENTS

PART 3: ALIVE—THE WHAT

APPENDICES

Pain is inevitable. Misery is a choice.

—Unknown

FOREWORD

I've known Kary—or PJ, as I call him—since he got out of divinity school and strolled into Grace Church Powell as our new youth pastor. He was 24 years old, he had at least *some* hair, and he was full of ideas, energy, and life.

We became friends almost in an instant. I was still working in the corporate world, but I already had one foot out the door. We had much in common even though we were eighteen years apart in age. We both had big dreams and seemingly even bigger fears.

You can relate, we know.

Fast forward a few years. I'd made the jump to start Built to Lead (BTL), and PJ would come to some of my "Friday Pastors" practices. He loved mixing it up intellectually and—I would later learn—physically too. These practices taught us both a ton.

We began to practice one-on-one as I took him on as a gratis coaching client. We worked on his BTL OPUS, and it brought clarity to his desire to write books—lots of books.

He started and finished his first one in the blink of an eye. He published it too. This should have been satisfying, but it wasn't. PJ had a deeper path buried within. He knew it in his head, but it hadn't quite made the journey to his heart.

We would talk about his labor and his love. He would offer up logical explanations for why the love had to wait and the labor had to dominate his day-to-day life. He would oftentimes work himself up into a lather about his situation and, after writing about it, come again to clarity in his head. But he couldn't quite muster up enough courage in his heart.

This pattern played out for years. We kept practicing. He kept learning without leaving.

Finally, I said something like, "You can't take the ring and stay in the Shire." (If you're unfamiliar with the metaphor, revisit *The Lord of the Rings*.)

PJ's heart was pierced. It was as if his deeper path suddenly opened up in front of him as clearly as it did for Dorothy when she discovered the yellow brick road and her hero's journey.

PJ left the Shire, grabbed his pen, and the rest is—as they say—history. Freakin' magic to see.

Today I have the privilege of standing beside this soul on fire named PJ. Faith has overwhelmed his fear. His big dream—his labor of love—has given him more courage and conviction. He doesn't even resemble the young man who once shook in fear at the thought of going it alone.

As you read his book, realize he wants you to do more than passively participate. PJ wants you to learn from his story and stop waiting to write yours. You too, friend, have a deeper path to discover.

My friend PJ will serve as your guide, but only for a while. There comes a point in all our journeys where we must go it alone. Take comfort in knowing this is part and parcel of the deeper path of discovery. Don't be afraid. Keep taking the baby steps forward. Keep moving through. It's what PJ and I are still doing. You can do it too.

Good work, my friend PJ. You have found your Deeper Path.

Keep working . . .

—Chet Scott, Founder of Built to Lead

A NOTE TO THE READER

Welcome to The Deeper Path.

Welcome to life change.

It might sound like a big claim, but I'm confident this book can change your life because the first life it changed was my own. When it was published in February 2012, I was a pastor entering my eleventh year at the same church. Three months later, I informed the church board I would be leaving. Six months after that, I said goodbye to everything familiar: a steady paycheck, health insurance, my colleagues, and comfort.

My departure wasn't reckless. After all, with a wife and three kids under six years old depending on me as the main financial provider, impulsivity wasn't even on my radar. My transition was an intentional decision to do my purpose full-time.

> CLARITY IS DANGEROUS. ONCE YOU KNOW WHAT YOU WANT, YOU'RE DISSATISFIED WITH ANYTHING LESS.

I often tell people that clarity is dangerous. Once you know what you want, you're dissatisfied with anything less. True, clarity comes with a cost, but the good news is it also comes with a big payoff. We call it the Deeper Path Payoff. Notice the progression below:

Clarity → Competence → Confidence → Influence → Impact → Income

WHY REPUBLISH THE BOOK?

Because *The Deeper Path* released many years ago, I wanted to update and expand it. Remember, when I first wrote the book, I was transitioning to do my purpose full-time. At that point, I still had the safety and familiarity of my day job, but I knew those days were numbered because clarity was on my side.

If you read the first edition, you witnessed my moments of bravery and my moments of fear and panic. By writing that initial manuscript, I was also literally writing my resignation letter. I knew it and I felt it.

I didn't remove those moments from this expanded and updated version. After all, you might still be in your day job surrounded by safety and familiarity. Maybe my fear and panic will bring you a kind of comfort too.

I didn't just stop there though. The truth is much has happened since 2012. First of all, I've found a wonderful group of friends. Together, we created a movement that has ignited over one million souls worldwide. We started a global team of hundreds of certified coaches, speakers, and trainers in dozens of countries. We even built a publishing company with over 500 authors, and it's growing every day.

In this edition, I share the most helpful lessons, stories, and tactics that I've learned along the way. After seven years, I've even rewritten my OPUS (which is listed in this book along with many other helpful tools). By the end of the book, you'll understand all about OPUS. And because you're brave, I'm betting you'll author your OPUS too. (More on that to come.)

For now, just show up filled up. Consume the content and apply the content. If you do, then like thousands of others who've taken The Deeper Path, you'll soon discover a simple method for finding clarity, mastering life, and doing your purpose every day.

I can't wait to hear about your life change.

Talk soon. And remember—I believe in you.

—Kary

INTRODUCTION

Those who turn back remember the ordeal.
Those who persevere remember the adventure.

—Milo Arnold

I'm writing this book with one hand: my left one. Nothing against the left-handed population—I respect and care for those people—but I'm right-handed, and I've written all my books with both hands. Except this one.

Seventeen years ago, something happened to me, although I didn't think too much of it at the time. The doctors finally caught it three months ago. As a result, I needed to have surgery. Up until that time, I was a "surgery virgin," but no longer.

While in wrestling practice back in high school, I attempted a move called a standing switch. Only I did it incorrectly, and my right shoulder paid the price. I didn't hear a tear, but I certainly felt one.

I remember yelling. It was a deep, genuine, from-the-belly yell. I hate those yells.

I don't like the word surgery either, which is why for seventeen years I ignored the pain in my shoulder. Avoiding it worked for a while, but in the back of my mind, I knew something was wrong. Sometimes, when things got too painful, I numbed the pain with over-the-counter meds, especially when playing sports.

Some people might debate whether it qualifies as a sport, but I enjoy the occasional round of disc golf. Looking back now, I realize my game always felt a little off. Certain throws produced a dull pain. I even stayed away from a few types of throws altogether because they made the pain worse.

My disc golf buddies never knew about my pain. I don't hang around people who make excuses, so I simply ignored the pain and avoided those particular throws for seventeen years.

Three months ago, all that changed.

Around Thanksgiving, my six-year-old son, brother-in-law, and father-in-law joined me in wintry Michigan for a game of disc golf. We came to a creek with a large pipe that spanned the ten-foot-wide stream of water.

Although there was a bridge for easy crossing, my adventurous son Keegan had a different idea. (We can't be too hard on him because his name means "little fiery one.") Rather excitedly, he asked if he could walk across on the pipe. I tossed some encouragement his way, and he sprang up and started walking across. I decided to join him as he crossed to the other side in case he hadn't quite mastered his balance yet.

He insisted he had learned this skill from Sensei Wu, the star of his favorite cartoon show at the time, *Lego Ninjago*. Still, his mother's warnings rang loud in my subconscious, so I assumed a supporting stance.

He made it halfway across and then started to teeter. Seeing his instability, my reflexes kicked in and I lunged for whatever body part I could grab. My right arm snatched him just in time. I managed to pull him awkwardly back onto the pipe.

We giggled, finished crossing, and doled out a round of high fives to his grandpa and uncle, witnesses to his bravery and our close call. If only we had walked away with just memories pumping through our brains and adrenaline pumping through our veins. Instead, I also carried with me a second tear in my shoulder. A week later, when I could no longer lift my arm, I knew I couldn't avoid the truth or the pain any longer.

I booked an appointment with a specialist to get a clearer picture of the damage.

The MRI didn't lie, and that winter my life changed in some unexpected ways. I experienced a surplus of medical bills, three months of physical therapy, lost days of work, a book deadline extension, the need to ask people for help, and—hardest of all for me—a ban from wrestling with my kids.

I learned a ton through the process. For starters, I discovered an unknown fear of mine. The MRI experience produced a severe claustrophobic reaction. I bet I looked odd kissing the ground after the technician pulled me out of the machine that day.

But I also learned that overcoming chronic pain—like a torn labrum—sometimes requires experiencing new kinds of pain—like surgery. I learned that sometimes our hurts are the only things that lead us to healing. If I hadn't received that second tear three months ago, I'd still be walking around ignorant of the initial tear from seventeen years ago.

Although I'm presently in pain and still healing, the truth is I no longer have two tears in my labrum. The surgeon repaired both and officially pronounced my shoulder as good as new.

Best of all, I'm told my disc golf game will be better than ever. And if all goes according to plan, I'm sure in a few short months I'll wonder why I waited so long.

Like me, you have pain in your life. We all do. But for most people, this pain may go unnoticed—for years.

We ignore the pain. We mask it. We numb it.

We get used to the limitations our pain brings, and we simply adjust.

We manage. We settle. We cope.

We live way below our abilities simply because we're unwilling to pursue the pain that would push us to reach our potential. We hide our hurts, and in the process, we sabotage our healing.

But it doesn't have to be this way. If we're willing—and brave—we can choose a Deeper Path.

And this Deeper Path makes all the difference.

> WE HIDE OUR HURTS, AND IN THE PROCESS, WE SABOTAGE OUR HEALING.

Before we celebrate this secret, we should first examine its price tag. Going beneath the surface comes with a cost, and the general population prefers to stay at ground level for a reason.

Anyone who engages in even the shallowest emotional excavation needs the right kind of equipment. To be strategic, we must get properly equipped before we begin digging. For this reason, we'll examine the why, the how, and the what of the Deeper Path.

Prepare to get a little messy—going five steps down tends to have that effect. But also expect some adventure too. Along the way, we'll meet a few brave souls—and a few crazy ones too.

My ultimate purpose in writing this book (left-handed, mind you) is that you become one of these few. You're too important not to be included in this elite class.

Ironically, to take The Deeper Path, we'll start by examining a specific takeoff. It might sound strange—go up to go down? Then again, the world we're about to explore may feel strange at first.

Even though the flight might get a little bumpy, I know you'll love where we land.

PART

ONE

Numb—The Why

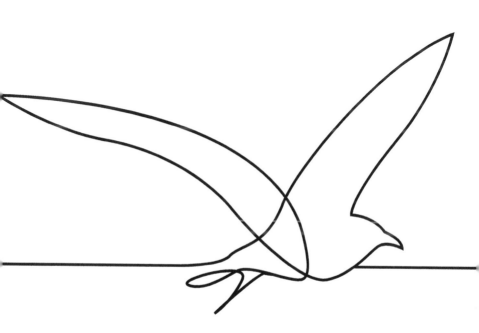

1

A ROUTINE TAKEOFF

I run on the road, long before I dance under the lights.

—Muhammad Ali

On January 15, 2009, the sun rose as on any other day. One hundred fifty-five people awoke, packed their bags, and said their goodbyes. They headed to the airport expecting nothing unusual—like most of us do on most of our days.

Lucky for them, they buckled in for the flight of their lives. Even luckier for them, their particular pilot would soon be touted as a hero on the evening news.

Everything started out rather predictably—the spiel from the flight attendants about wearing the oxygen masks in the case of an emergency, the reminder to fasten their safety belts, the semi-awkward attempt to greet the stranger in the adjacent seat. Minutes later the plane raced down the runway and became airborne, along with musings about the day that now lay spread out for the seizing.

Like clockwork, the clock worked the way it should, bringing routine right along with it. Fortunately, this particular routine proved to be exceptionally routine, creating potential space for reading, writing, and even dozing for a few sleepy souls.

But only ninety seconds into the flight, the pilot noticed an unexpected obstacle. Or more accurately, unexpected *obstacles*. Birds suddenly filled his view.

Lots of birds. Lots of *big* birds.

In his book *Highest Duty*, Captain Chesley "Sully" Sullenberger explains that the Canada geese with six-foot wingspans, weighing eight to eighteen pounds each, sounded like large hail pelting the plane. Moments later he felt what every pilot fears—double engine failure resulting from a brutal bird strike.[1]

Routine had suddenly been blown to pieces—along with the birds.

The plane lost thrust and, given its low speed and low altitude over New York City, one of the most densely populated areas on the planet, Captain Sully knew he sat front and center in a seriously challenging situation.

Although he had never requested this experience, in that instant, life sought his response. And 154 people prayed that Captain Sully's response would prove to be the right one.

We all have at least one defining moment in our lifetime. Many of us have a handful more. We can't predict them. And we can't create them—at least not easily.

But defining moments are coming for us. They will hunt us down and find us. They're not for us or against us. They simply are. They're a mirror—a complex combination of circumstances meant to do one solitary thing—reveal us. What's inside of us is going to come out. And whether we welcome our response or whether we'd like to reverse time and bury our response right back where it came from, know this. The world is watching.

We were going to see Captain Sully on the evening news that January day. Regardless of the pilot's actions following the unlucky bird strike, his number had come up, and life had decided to snatch him from semi-anonymity and thrust him onto center stage.

Through a series of events he couldn't avoid, Captain Sully faced his defining moment. And he faced it without the luxury of creating a plan.

Nope. Life happened, and he didn't have time for anything except an immediate response. But this is precisely what made Captain Sully a hero. And he didn't need a bird strike to tell him that. He already knew the secret that sets people like him apart from the rest. He acknowledged the reality that is no respecter of persons, race, age, intelligence, income, or education. He knew The Deeper Path and, more importantly, he traveled The Deeper Path.

Unfortunately, although this truth is available to all, it's understood by only a few. And despite this truth lurking in the shadows on most days, every so often, like on January 15, 2009, life decides to invite it into our awareness, even if for only a brief moment.

But what if we could tease this truth out of hiding, study it, and use it to our advantage? What if we could make it work for us and not against us? That wouldn't be fair, now, would it?

Like me, you've probably been sold the same claustrophobic cliché your entire life: *life isn't fair.* Well, what if in this situation it was? What if the universe operates according to specific laws and Sully simply used them to his advantage?

Think about it. Most people accept the law of gravity. Despite our best intentions, if we step off a cliff, we're going to fall and crash at the bottom. This law is no respecter of persons either—unless we have a hang glider, jetpack, parachute, or some other invention strapped to our back. To keep ourselves from falling, we would have to know the law and put it to work for ourselves.

What if bending laws is exactly what Captain Sully did? What if we could follow suit and bend laws too—leveraging them and making them work for us, not against us?

Imagine the possibilities.

We could shortcut heartaches, ensure successes, and take strides ahead of our competition. We could excel in relationships, avoid emotional blowups, and increase our impact in the world.

We could also choose our response ahead of time and guarantee that our defining moments would define us exactly the way we desired.

Unfortunately, many people want none of it. To admit the existence of The Deeper Path is to admit the need to interact with it. This is precisely why most people consider January 15, 2009, a fluke—an example of luck in its purest form. Many prefer to label the whole experience as a miracle. And that's just what they did—classifying this event as the "Miracle on the Hudson."[2]

But this wasn't a miracle—though I do believe in miracles. Sully achieved "the most successful ditching in aviation history" without luck or chance on his side.[3]

Was he a hero?

You bet, and the rest of the crew with him. They rightfully received the highest award. But this "miracle" wasn't simply happenstance. Rather, this successful emergency landing on the Hudson River resulted from a series of decisions determined long before and birthed out of something much deeper.

As Captain Sully told CBS news anchor Katie Couric, "For 42 years, I've been making small, regular deposits in this bank of experience: education and training. And on January 15 the balance was sufficient so that I could make a very large withdrawal."[4]

Know this. Your number will come up. I can't tell you the exact time of your defining moment, but trust me, it's coming. And it doesn't care if you're ready.

Now our friends and family, they do care. They're rooting for our success, and they want us to land safely. But let's be honest. They have a vested interest too. None of us is flying alone. We all have passengers with us. They're belted in behind us, praying that our response will prove to be the right one.

> I CAN'T TELL YOU THE EXACT TIME OF YOUR DEFINING MOMENT, BUT TRUST ME, IT'S COMING.

But this is much bigger than even the "passengers" directly connected to us. US Airways Flight 1549 landed in the Hudson River adjacent to midtown Manhattan. Thousands of innocent New Yorkers were engaged in their normal routines that day, completely oblivious to the mass of metal with full fuel tanks descending directly on top of them.

Both our action and our inaction directly and indirectly affect our world.

The choice is ours. Do we want to shake the dice and wait for our unexpected bird strike before we determine our response? If Captain Sully had waited, he, the crew, the passengers, and the plane would have gone down in flames like other flights before his.[5]

The world is waiting on you to get past what you're waiting for. We need you to convert your apprehension into energy. We need you to take The Deeper Path. Tomorrow could be your defining moment, the day when your number is drawn.

Use today to prepare for tomorrow.

Know that we're behind you.

And we want you to land safely.

Because we have a vested interest in your success.

2

THE MELODY LINE

It's a beautiful day, don't let it get away.

—U2

F ans of the Dublin-based rock band U2 can probably
recall the melody line of the song "Beautiful Day" without a second thought. Melody lines wield that kind of
power and potential.

As we might expect, Bono, the humanitarian and main
vocalist of U2, is often linked with the term *melody line*. He's
a singer, after all, and for one of the biggest rock bands of
all time.

If you're a nonmusical person like me, you might not know
the technical meaning of *melody line*. With a little digging, I
discovered it's "a linear succession of musical tones perceived
as a single entity."[1]

Bono created an alternative definition for melody line
around the same time he cofounded ONE, a grassroots advo-
cacy and campaigning organization. ONE fights extreme
poverty and preventable disease, particularly in Africa, by
raising public awareness and pressuring political leaders to

support smart and effective policies and programs that are saving lives, helping to put kids in school, and improving futures.[2]

ONE boasts a big vision, but the billion-dollar question is "How does someone make that vision stick?" David Lane, ONE's chief executive officer and former executive director of the Bill and Melinda Gates Foundation, labored closely with Bono to discover the answer.

In their book *Why Are We Bad at Picking Good Leaders?*, authors Jeffery Cohn and Jay Moran take us deeper into the minds of Bono and Lane and deeper into the metaphor of melody lines.

Bono and Lane constantly honed their message, what they referred to as "the melody line." In musical terms, a melody line is a series of rising or falling notes that gives a song its recognizable theme. It's the part of the song that a listener remembers, the notes that stand out above the rest. Bono and Lane turned this into a metaphor for giving voice to their organization's big ideas.[3]

WHAT'S YOUR BIG IDEA?

Bono's not the only one with a big idea. You have one too—though at the moment it may still be buried deep inside you. By taking The Deeper Path, you'll discover your own melody line and your big idea.

Ideas are powerful. They can change the world. We observe this in Leonardo DiCaprio's character Cobb from the film *Inception*. Although the story is fiction, Cobb's commentary on ideas is couched in truth.

In the movie, Cobb explains, "What's the most resilient parasite? An idea. A single idea from the human mind can build cities. An idea can transform the world and rewrite all the rules."[4]

Melody lines and ideas are interrelated because melody lines give voice to our big ideas. A message without a voice is simply a thought. But a message with too many voices is simply a noise.

Before we dig too deep, first, a little something about our trip. Pain is inevitable. I always appreciate doctors or dentists who give me a heads-up. The phrase "this is going to sting a little" always went a long way in building trust, even when I was a kid. The professionals who simply stuck me without warning failed to earn my trust. I ended up resenting them, even if their motivation was to protect me from the truth.

Tell me the ouch is coming, and then I can prepare.

So, in an attempt to earn your trust, take this as my advance warning. If you keep reading, pain will appear in your immediate future. It has to. Our path can't be pain-free because life isn't.

We humans take great measures to insulate and isolate ourselves from pain. This is our model from infancy. I remember driving each one of our newborn babies home from the hospital. Though they were buckled into a protective car seat and surrounded by four walls of airbags, twenty miles per hour still felt too fast to me. My wife, Kelly, and I cushioned their reality, pushing pain out the door.

But given enough time, pain eventually breaks through and corners us. When it does, most of us run for cover. We numb ourselves because when we're numb we don't feel anything—the good or the bad. We shout for our savior named noise to come rescue us and drown out our ache.

Unfortunately, by numbing our pain we also numb our potential.

Life gives us plenty of escape buttons to press when we feel our pain mounting. These distractions and diversions serve as coping strategies and survival tactics. Seventeenth-century French philosopher Blaise Pascal observed them and accurately forewarned us of their lethal effects.

"The only thing that consoles us for our miseries is distraction,
yet that is the greatest of our wretchednesses. Because that is

what mainly prevents us from thinking about ourselves and leads us imperceptibly to damnation. Without it we should be bored, and boredom would force us to search for a firmer way out, but distraction entertains us and leads us imperceptibly to death."[5]

Pascal believed that boredom would eventually lead to our escape. On the flip side, he also believed anesthetizing our pain unconsciously invites mediocrity.

I wonder what Pascal would think of our distractions today. Spending endless hours plugged into video games, excavating Facebook statuses, and binging on the latest series, leaves us unfulfilled. Vicariously living through someone else's life—via reality TV—always leaves us wanting more.

We're spirit, not just flesh. We're meant to show up present in our own lives. We're meant to be fully alive, not half dead. We're designed for a fuller expression and fuller expansion of what we currently know. We long for more—more resources to share, more compassion to give, more fulfillment to experience, more purpose to taste, more peace to feel, and more joy to spread.

> WE'RE MEANT TO BE FULLY ALIVE, NOT HALF DEAD.

Despite all this, we're deathly afraid, and we embody the "F" word—FEAR.

We resist traveling anyplace we've never been because on those roads we don't know the way. We want a map, a compass, and a GPS, but we forget that the richest roads are unpaved and unknown.

Maybe this is why *The Fellowship of the Ring* resonates with so many people. We see ourselves as common and unimpressive, just like the two hobbits Sam and Frodo. We fail to realize that our own courage can only poke through when we get outside our comfort zone.

Frodo heard the melody line before Sam and brought it to his attention:

Sam: This is it.

Frodo: This is what?

Sam: If I take one more step, it'll be the farthest away from home I've ever been.

Frodo: Come on, Sam. Remember what Bilbo used to say: "It's a dangerous business, Frodo, going out your door. You step onto the road, and if you don't keep your feet, there's no knowing where you might be swept off to."[6]

These two predictable hobbits needed to leave the "comfort of home," because that comfort was slowly killing them. There's nothing wrong with home, but if we're honest, most of us are strangers in our own homes.

We're homesick for a place we've never been.

Home isn't a bad place, but we often ask too much of it. We hope it answers all our aches. But home is a metaphor for where we've been, not a place we're going. Home can be a prison if it's a place devoid of growth.

A while back, my friend Chet Scott made a deeply profound and painful point to me. Chet is the founder of an unconventional company called Built to Lead.[7] Although some might try to label Chet a "life coach," he would beg to differ. Chet's heart is to build his clients by breaking them down—often through pain.

Chet warned me with searing truth, "You can't take the ring *and* stay in the Shire."

Ouch!

I wanted to do both simultaneously. I convinced myself safety and risk could be married. I believed comfort and adventure were compatible. Chet disagreed, and loved me enough to call me out. To go up, I needed to give up.

This strategy requires confronting all kinds of deep issues. Like failure, competence, risk, and reward.

The first place we need to travel is deep inside ourselves—uncharted and untamed. Henry Stanley Haskins accurately observed, "What lies behind us and what lies before us are tiny matters compared to what lies within us."[8]

We need to feel our own pain. And we must understand our own story if we hope to help other people find theirs.

So let me put it back on you.

What's your melody line? And what's your big idea?

Like every other outlier I've met, I know it involves taking "a ring" of sorts.

But to do that, you're going to have to leave "the Shire."

The next question only you can answer. Are you ready to open the door to a brand-new world?

3

LEAVING THE NURSERY

God whispers to us in our pleasures, speaks in our conscience, but shouts in our pains; it is His megaphone to rouse a deaf world.

—C. S. Lewis

We never had one in our house growing up. It wasn't the price that kept us away. I think my parents just never bought one. As a result, it wasn't until our ninth year of marriage that my wife finally purchased one. Ironically, one week later we ended up purchasing three more. Now we'd never be without one—if we can steal them away from our kids. Just the other day, I came downstairs and saw our little daughter cuddled up in one. She's a smart girl who knows a good thing when she sees it—or in this case, she knows a good thing when she feels it.

She loves her new electric blanket.

We live in Ohio, so at times the winter season can get a little chilly. Now, with the flip of a switch, we get instant heat whenever we want.

Electric blankets aren't our enemy. Comfort, however, can be. Consider the fact: Most mornings, most people struggle to emerge from a warm, soft bed devoid of noise and distraction. Most of the population hits the snooze button multiple times. We prefer swimming in a sea of sheets rather than showing up filled up ready for life.

But why?

When you were conceived, you started in a warm, soft environment devoid of noise and distraction. Residing in a sac of safety and swimming in a sea of fluid, you were comfortably insulated and isolated. Your body felt the rhythm of your mother, and you rested in your unawareness.

Eventually, your birth day came, the day you entered a new world. Pain served as the catalyst for your new birth and propelled you from what you knew out into the vast unknown.

With each passing day, you became more and more acquainted with pain—the pain of hunger, of feeling scared, of being alone.

Many of us have experienced our caretakers' desire to protect us from this pain. As best they could, they created a specific environment, better known as a nursery.

Nurseries vary in size and scope. Some are gigantic, outfitted with plush carpet and impressive mobiles. Others are quaint, painted with calming colors on all sides. Regardless of their size, most nurseries are designed with one specific goal in mind: safety. Baby wipe warmers, stuffed creatures, outlet covers, monitors, blankets, night-lights, cribs—all this pain protection hardwired into our lives from an early age.

Thankfully, a few kind people took some measures of safety in your life. If they hadn't, you might not be reading this book, (especially if they forgot those outlet covers).

But this desire for a pain-free world doesn't go away later in life. No wonder as adults we feel at peace swimming in a sea of sheets, savoring that snooze button, sleeping carefree and enjoying electric blankets. No wonder our warm, soft environment keeps us from activity.

There's nothing wrong with pain-free experiences. The problem occurs when our aspirations rank no higher than insulating and isolating ourselves from discomfort. The problem occurs when we fixate on remaining in the nursery.

We were never meant to live out our days inside the nursery. We were meant for more—much more.

God knows the only thing that propels us from the nursery. And if God didn't allow it in our lives, odds are we'd never choose it.

"What's the universal emotion?"

Chet asked me this interesting question a few years back.

Not quite understanding the question, I asked him to clarify.

"You know, the one feeling that every single person has experienced."

It took me a moment to locate my answer. "Love," I suggested. "Everyone has experienced love."

Chet shook his head.

"Loneliness?"

"Nope."

"Fear."

"No."

"OK, then, pain. Every single person has experienced pain," I said. A smile slowly found its way onto Chet's face.

"Exactly."

Think about it. Pain is the first feeling we express when we arrive in this world. And it's the last feeling most of us experience when we leave this world.

If a baby *doesn't* come out crying, medical professionals get worried and rush to discover what's wrong. Chances are, this lack of response results from a deeper pain lurking beneath the surface.

Most of us have a jacked-up view of pain. We believe it's bad and that it should be avoided at all costs. Lies like this go down easily because most of us don't have an alternative definition of pain to challenge such beliefs.

Fortunately, the medical community offers some: Pain is an uncomfortable feeling and/or an unpleasant sensation in the body. The presence of pain is often an indication that something is wrong.[1]

Some interesting applications emerge from this definition.

- Pain should be examined more closely to discover the deeper issue.

- Pain is merely an indication that something is wrong.

- Pain shouldn't be avoided.

- Pain isn't the problem.

- Pain is a symptom.

These same professionals go further by classifying pain into two categories: chronic and acute.

Chronic Pain: This type of pain persists despite the fact the injury has healed. Pain signals remain active in the nervous system for weeks, months, or years. Some people suffer chronic pain in the absence of any past injury or evidence of body damage.

Acute Pain: This type of pain begins suddenly and is usually sharp in quality. It serves as a warning of disease or a threat to the body. In most cases, acute pain does not last longer than six months, and it disappears when the underlying cause of pain has been treated or has healed.[6] Within our conversation, more thoughts emerge that are critical if we want to understand more about ourselves and our world. First, most of us don't want pain, but unless we learn how to deal with our pain, our only other option is to numb it. And regrettably, we live in a world that numbs it well.

> UNLESS WE LEARN HOW TO DEAL WITH OUR PAIN, OUR ONLY OTHER OPTION IS TO NUMB IT.

Second, all this pain is an indication that something is deeply wrong. Such pain isn't good or bad—it simply *is*. Pain *becomes* good or bad based on what we do with it. Good pain is essential, and unless it's permitted—in many cases even pursued—then bad pain will triumph and have its way.

Bad Pain: Extensive suffering that is chronic and purposeless. Bad pain leads to a state of unproductive inaction and ultimately a type of serious injury or death.

Good Pain: Intentional hurt that is acute and purposeful. Good pain leads to productive action and ultimately a type of healing or resurrection.

Think about your own life for a moment.

Which situations contain bad pain? Which situations contain good pain?

If we can't discern the difference, we'll tend to label them both negatively and dismiss them promptly, sending the good pain packing.

If you've ever experienced real relationship, then you've experienced real pain. Such was the case for world-renowned writer and professor C. S. Lewis. His mother's death from cancer when he was only a boy reshaped his entire life. Pain walled him in, preventing Lewis from venturing into other relationships. He reasoned that a life of love meant a life of pain, and regrettably he reasoned that such a life wasn't worth it.

C. S. Lewis probably wouldn't have been a fan of the now-famous line from nineteenth-century poet Alfred, Lord

Tennyson: "'Tis better to have loved and lost than never to have loved at all."

Lewis gained a prominent position as a professor at Oxford and held it for over thirty years, and within the academy he ruled the roost. His brilliant mind and sharp humor ensured him the upper hand in professional encounters with colleagues and students. His intellect allowed him the ability to "school" any other educational opponent.

Lewis's books and writings became the context in which he explored other types of relationships. In his fictional characters, he found complete control. His world of writing granted him godlike attributes: omniscience, omnipresence, and omnipotence.

But Lewis soon discovered that books can't talk back to you. Books can't embrace or engage you the same way a person can. His need for relationships became too great. Finally, love found him.

An American writer, Joy Gresham, came crashing into his life and brought love with her. Lewis and Gresham began a relationship and eventually married. Lewis felt alive and free, just as he did before his mother passed so many years prior.

But when Lewis opened the door of his heart to love, pain snuck in as well. Only a few years into their marriage, Gresham suffered from the same disease that stole Lewis's mother decades before. When she died, so did a piece of Lewis's heart.

The movie *Shadowlands* captures this love story between Lewis and Gresham well. The emotional scenes include some incredibly insightful dialogue by Anthony Hopkins, who plays C. S. Lewis in the film. In one of those verbal exchanges, he brushes up against The Deeper Path.

Isn't God supposed to be good? Isn't He supposed to love us? Does God want us to suffer? What if the answer to that question is "yes"? I suggest to you that it is because God loves us that He makes us the gift of suffering.

I'm not sure that God wants us to be happy. I think He wants us to be able to love and be loved. He wants us to grow up. We think our childish toys bring us all the happiness there is and our nursery is the whole wide world. But something must drive us out of the nursery to the world of others, and that something is suffering.[2]

Within our lives, although we may crave the comfort of those cozy blankets, pain is God's gift to push us out of the nursery. No wonder we feel unrest. We want to heal, but we don't want to hurt. We want love, but we don't want pain.

And so we enter relationships with flimsy masks comprised of faulty demands and forced commands. We want a shadow of love, but we don't want authentic love. This is why it's so hard for us to understand God. We can't wrap our arms around how a good, all-powerful God can coexist in a world of pain. We buy into a misbelief—that love can exist without pain. But authentic love and pain must coexist.

Authentic love led C. S. Lewis to care for Joy Gresham when she suffered from the same tragic disease that took his mother's life. Authentic love held Jesus's wrists to the tree as he took on the sin of the world. And authentic love serves as the glue in your relationships, despite the unavoidable pain they contain.

But if we're honest, we still struggle. Knowing the truth doesn't make accepting that truth any easier.

May I ask?

Where are you still white-knuckled clinging to the illusion of the nursery? Where are you insulating and isolating your heart to avoid the hurt? How are you running from the relationship with yourself? With others?

As a poster child from the nursery, I understand the logic of remaining there. It seems safer, cleaner, and more inviting.

But it's not. It's an illusion. And that's all it is.

You know this. You feel this.

You've understood it for quite some time. This is what makes you different: the reality that you're willing to explore life outside the nursery. And this little difference sets you apart. But there's more to this little difference than what we can see. We need to dig even deeper below the surface.

4

THE LITTLE DIFFERENCE

You must strive to find your own voice.
Because the longer you wait to begin, the less
likely you are to find it at all.

—John Keating, *Dead Poets Society*

I've always wondered what separates one person from the next.

In athletic championships, when adversity strikes, one athlete rises to the challenge and another athlete falters under pressure. In business setbacks, one leader rallies her department and another one self-destructs. In economic difficulties, one family works together under the banner of unity and another family fights each other and goes down in flames.

The same team, the same organization, the same neighborhood, but entirely different results.

In their book *212° The Extra Degree*, authors Sam Parker and Mac Anderson expand upon this "little difference," referring to it as "the extra degree."

"At 211° water is hot. At 212°, it boils. And with boiling

water, comes steam. And steam can power a locomotive. The one extra degree makes the difference."[1]

The authors provide several other examples of "the extra degree" within the world of sports:

1. The margin of victory in the men's 800-meter race in the 1984 Summer Olympic Games was only 0.71 seconds—less than one second.

2. The average margin of victory in the Daytona 500 and the Indianapolis 500 (combined) over a ten-year period was 1.54 seconds. And the prize money for second place is less than half of that for first place.

3. The average margin of victory for the last twenty-five years in all major PGA golf tournaments combined was less than three strokes.[2]

Although these observations provide interesting trivia tidbits, the bigger question is the story behind "the extra degree." And even more relevant to our context: How is this degree quantified when it comes to people? It's one thing to win a race. It's another thing to overcome chronic personal pain.

Bottom line: What can we credit for "the little difference"?

Some tip their hat to simple perseverance. Thomas Edison said, "Many of life's failures are men who did not realize how close they were to success when they gave up."

Examining Edison's life closer, we see a never-give-up attitude. As the story goes, Edison was asked why he failed so many times when trying to create the first light bulb. He is famously quoted as replying, "I have not failed ten thousand times. I have successfully discovered ten thousand ways that it will not work."

Regardless of the complete accuracy of the story, we should question if simple perseverance was Edison's secret.

Me? I don't buy it. It might read kindly in a greeting card, but you can't take it to the bank. Clichés don't convert into cash.

I bet people taught you the same warmed-over clichés they taught me. See if you can finish these statements.

1. No Pain, no _____.

2. Winners never quit, and quitters never _____.

3. If you can dream it, you can do _____.

4. No guts, no _____.

5. The early bird gets the _____.

6. It's not what you know, it's who you _____.

7. Be at the right place at the right _____

Funny how much these phrases shape our ideology and direct our actions, many times even indirectly. Although a tiny nugget of truth might reside within each phrase, breaking them down reveals some interesting false assumptions.

NO PAIN, NO GAIN.

Key point: Hard work.
False assumption: Pain produces promotion.
Truth: Choosing the right pain produces promotion.
Story: I know people who work incredibly hard, never reach their potential, and die with their music still inside them.

WINNERS NEVER QUIT, AND QUITTERS NEVER WIN.

Key point: Persistence.
False assumption: Stick with something long enough and you will win.

Truth: Healthy self-awareness of one's strengths and weaknesses combined with persistence can convert into winning.
Story: I know people who never gave up their dream but failed to acknowledge they were completely unqualified to achieve it.

IF YOU CAN DREAM IT, YOU CAN DO IT.

Key point: Imagination.
False assumption: Imagination guarantees you will achieve what you want.
Truth: Vision is only the first step in possibly achieving what you want.
Story: I know people who have an unlimited number of ideas that never amount to anything.

NO GUTS, NO GLORY.

Key point: Risk.
False assumption: Risk will yield reward.
Truth: The right risk at the right time in the right way with the right people will yield reward.
Story: I know people who take all kinds of risks and simply take recklessness with them wherever they go.

THE EARLY BIRD GETS THE WORM.

Key point: Scarcity.
False assumption: There is only one worm.
Truth: A mindset of scarcity, fear, and competition will produce a toxic attitude of threat and defensiveness.
Story: I know people who rush to take first and are in last place because of it.

IT'S NOT WHAT YOU KNOW, IT'S WHO YOU KNOW.

Key point: Luck.
False assumption: You can blame your plateau on a person you don't even know yet.
Truth: Before others will choose to believe in you, they will naturally judge if you believe in yourself.
Story: I know people who emitted the right frequency and attracted the right people to them because of it.

BE AT THE RIGHT PLACE AT THE RIGHT TIME.

Key point: Chance.
False assumption: You stumble into greatness when you stumble into the right space.
Truth: If you've prepared for the moment, then the moment is prepared for you.

> IF YOU'VE PREPARED FOR THE MOMENT, THEN THE MOMENT IS PREPARED FOR YOU.

Story: I know people who won while in the wrong place at the wrong time and others who lost when they were in the right place at the right time.

Although mining these myths proves helpful, it's still not enough. And if "the extra degree" even escapes these clichés, where can we find it? No one can deny its existence, but can we capture it long enough to examine it with the hope of mastering its genius?

Sometimes this "little difference" surfaces when traumatic events pop into our awareness through the nightly news. One of these events occurred on an otherwise typical day in January 2011.

Although you might not have agreed with her public policies, if you heard her story, your heart went out to former Congresswoman Gabrielle Giffords of Arizona who survived an attempt on her life. Others were not so lucky. The shooter, Jared Loughner, killed six people and wounded thirteen more. Tragically, his youngest victim was a nine-year-old girl.

Because the shooter fired his gun from less than three feet away, sending a bullet straight through Giffords's brain, her future looked grim.[3] A portion of her skull the size of her palm had to be removed due to the swelling in her brain.

Grave predictions from professionals emerged rather quickly. Former surgeon general Dr. Richard Carmona said, "With guarded optimism, I hope she will survive, but this is a very devastating wound."[4]

Severe brain injuries rarely produce anything but grief and tragedy, and less than 10 percent of people with brain injuries even survive. Gabby Giffords not only survived, but she is also making a strong comeback, even today. She and her husband, Mark Kelly, an astronaut and captain in the United States Navy, chronicled their painstaking journey in a book titled *Gabby: A Story of Courage and Hope*.

Mark lets us into their world when he vulnerably writes:

I used to be able to tell just what my wife, Gabby, was thinking. She was a woman who lived in the moment—every moment. Gabby was a talker, too. Gabby doesn't have all those words at her command anymore, at least not yet. A brain injury like hers is a kind of hurricane blowing away some words and phrases, and leaving others almost within reach, but buried deep, under debris or in a different place.[5]

In Mark's own words, Gabby's voice was buried deep and needed to be excavated. She wanted so badly to move on with life. She was lucky to be alive, but her recovery progressed rather slowly, at times making her feel less than lucky. Her life had changed dramatically and she couldn't just quickly move on.

In a real way, by losing her physical speech, Gabby also lost her figurative voice. She suffers from expressive aphasia, a disorder caused by damage to or developmental issues in anterior regions of the brain. Expressive aphasia blocks the ability to produce written or spoken language. Although sufferers cognitively know what they want to say, their brains cannot retrieve the correct words. Often frustration, grief, and depression set in.

But neither Gabby nor Mark has given up easily. Gabby is slowly finding her voice again, and ironically, it's directly tied to her finding her melody line, both literally and figuratively.

A LITERAL MELODY LINE

Given the nature of her story and the political ramifications involved, it's no surprise that in order to get Gabby back on track, Mark and other loved ones called upon many of the best experts around the world. However, one particular type of expert they chose might surprise you: a music therapist.

Singing in a time of overwhelming pain? You bet. We can trick the brain by singing first and talking second. Music therapists tell us that when we sing we retrieve pitch, melody, and rhythm. Although language is normally held in the left side of the brain, music exists in both hemispheres.

"Music is that other road to get back to language," said Megan Morrow, Giffords's music therapist and a certified brain injury specialist at TIRR Memorial Hermann Rehabilitation Hospital in Houston, Texas. Morrow compared the process to a freeway detour. "You aren't able to go forward on that pathway anymore," she said, but "you can exit and go around, and get to where you need to go."[6]

Music helps many people get unstuck. Skeptically, some of us might wonder how someone can sing but not speak.

Dr. Oliver Sacks, professor of neurology and psychiatry at Columbia University, provides some insight. "Nothing activates the brain so extensively as music . . . and brain imagery . . . showed it had been possible to create a new language area on the right side of the brain . . . and that blew my mind."

Ever seen the movie *Awakenings*? Dr. Oliver Sacks's work with Parkinson's disease spurred both the film and the eponymous book. He tells us, "These patients 'have some words somewhere,' but must be 'tricked or seduced into discovering them.'"[7]

Melodic intonation therapy (MIT) is the technical term for this therapeutic process used by music therapists and speech pathologists to help patients with communication disorders caused by brain damage. This method uses a style of singing called melodic intonation to stimulate activity in the right hemisphere of the brain, which assists in speech production.

MIT was inspired by the observation that individuals with expressive aphasia sometimes can sing words or phrases that they normally cannot speak. The goal of melodic intonation therapy is to utilize singing to access the language-capable regions in the right hemisphere and use those regions to compensate for lost function in the left hemisphere. Because patients are better at singing phrases than speaking them, the natural musical component of speech is used to engage patients' ability to voice phrases.

Notice the amazing pattern.

Gabby first found her melody line.

Singing this melody line helped her remember her song.

And by remembering her song, she remembered her words.

And when Gabby remembered her words, then she rediscovered her voice.

In a literal sense, this process helps Gabby recover, but this process works in the figurative sense as well.

A FIGURATIVE MELODY LINE

Only weeks after Gabby's initial injury, Mark began presenting his wife with small goals, asking her how many fingers he held up or to recall simple memories. Mark believes hope is a form of love, and therefore, overcoming small challenges could produce small victories and with them small doses of hope.

As time marched on, so did their recovery from an incredibly traumatic event. Mark embodies courage on many fronts, including commanding the final mission of the Space Shuttle Endeavour less than five months after his wife's injury.

Asked to describe Mark in one word, Gabby chose "Brave."

Gabby embodies a bit of bravery herself. On August 1, 2011, less than eight months after the assassination attempt, she returned to Capitol Hill to make an appearance and received a warm bipartisan welcome from her colleagues on the House floor.

Having known much of her backstory, I sat stunned by the video footage of her appearance. Her "little difference" injected energy into the room that day. Electric and contagious, her courage did exactly what all courage is meant to do: inspire others.

Representative Jeff Flake said, "The two times that stand out in my mind—my whole memory of my time in Congress—is singing 'God Bless America' with people on 9/11 on the east steps [of the US Capitol] and then when Gabby Giffords walked in the chambers on August 1."[8]

How does someone in a matter of months go from speechless and sprawled out on a hospital bed to standing tall and speaking on the House floor on Capitol Hill? What is this "one degree" that sets Gabby Giffords apart from many other brain injury sufferers?

Unmistakably, it's because she found her voice. Watching her extensive interview with Diane Sawyer of *ABC News*, I learned that quite intentionally one particular phrase made it on her practice list for speech therapy: "I will return."

And herein lies another glimpse of The Deeper Path: her cross is bigger than her crown.

This is the same secret we observed in Captain Sully's ordeal earlier. And this is the same secret that enables me the privilege of writing you this book right now. Presently, one of these two orientations is pumping through your veins. Either your cross is bigger than your crown, or your crown is bigger than your cross.

You might not comprehend the magnitude of this subtle distinction right now, but you will. This "little difference" makes all the difference. In a manner of speaking, it is *the* difference maker.

Before we dig deep into the cross and crown distinction, let's close the loop on Gabby. Like any good excavator, we want to know how it all turned out. Did she serve another term? Is she presently in office? How is she now?

Although Representative Gabby Giffords announced her resignation on January 22, 2012, she still clings to her crown. Intently, I watched the video in which she regrettably announced to her state and the world that her time in public office had ended. Here's what she said:

> Arizona is my home, always will be. A lot has happened over the past year. We cannot change that. But I know on the issues we fought for we can change things for the better. Jobs, border security, veterans. We can do so much more by working together. I don't remember much from that horrible day, but I will never forget the trust you placed in me to be your voice. Thank you for your prayers and for giving me time to recover. I have more work to do on my recovery so to do what is best for Arizona I will step down this week.[9]

She closed the video by saying, "I'm getting better. Every day, my spirit is high. I will return and we will work together for Arizona and this great country."[10]

That melody line, again: "I will return."

That's the same phrase we heard in her speech therapy. Because she clarified her crown and because she clings to that crown, she has the courage to carry her cross. Knowing the little bit that I do about Gabby, I'd say she's not setting that cross down anytime soon. Gabby understands the Law of the Crown: when we see our crown clearly, we can carry our cross willingly.

Her resignation shocked many who knew Gabby's resolve and determination. She embodied courage, and courage can't be contained because it's infectious.

Fellow Arizona Democrat Representative Raul Grijalva was surprised by Giffords's resignation. "I thought she would just see how the recovery proceeded, but I guess she decided in her own mind that this recovery is number one and that's the right decision for her," he said.[11]

Her growing fan club now carries her cross with her, and sometimes even for her. On days when she might not feel strong, her community fills in the gaps. This is the unavoidable byproduct of a clarified crown. People see it and, just as important, they hear it too.

We hear Gabby's song because we hear her voice. And many of us sing her song with her and for her, even in dark moments such as her resignation.

"She will fully recover and when she decides to come back from her pause to take care of herself, she'll pick up where she left off, there's no question about that," Grijalva said. "I'm looking forward to seeing her, thanking her, wishing her the best, and letting her know we're going to keep the seat warm for her."[12]

Gabby now embodies an idea much bigger than a political party. She transcended Congress and even politics by connecting with something every human faces: pain.

THE CROSS AND THE CROWN

I heard it while watching *The Passion of the Christ*. Although the melody line came through clear, the application was a little foggy at first.

In the crucifixion scene, one of the thieves on the cross next to Jesus mocks him.

"Why do you embrace your cross, you fool?" the criminal asks.

Good question.

Why would someone embrace something as painful as a cross?

But it's just a movie, right? Make-believe? Jesus didn't really view his cross that way. Did he?

The author of the book of Hebrews clears up any confusion: "Let us fix our eyes on Jesus, the author and perfecter of our faith, who for the joy set before him endured the cross."

Joy about a cross?

Today, we beautify them. We wear them in our ears and around our necks. We see crosses in our places of worship and we find them in our art. We display them as a symbol of hope and inspiration.

Not so in the first century. Crosses were instruments of death. Crosses lined roadways, pathways, and walkways. They guaranteed certain sounds, like deep moans of anguish from people suffocating to death. Crosses brought with them an undeniable stench—the smell of rotting corpses. And they invited certain images, like circling vultures fed on decomposing flesh.

The Romans were smart people, utilizing crosses as motivation for accepting Roman control. They created them to inject a fear factor into their society. Crosses were a daily reminder to everyone about the result of rebellion. With the purpose of generating unquestioning allegiance, the Romans created the perfect killing machine.

So why would anyone welcome this instrument of suffering?

Today, it would be like expressing affection for an electric chair. We don't see too many people wearing that as jewelry or portraying it in art. Electric chairs hardly conjure up feelings of hope and inspiration.

But Jesus tapped into another reality. He saw the importance of the cross because he saw past it. He had crystal clear clarity for his crown. And he knew his cross was the only way to achieve his crown. So it became his passion and he carried it willingly, even joyfully.

Experts generally define the word *passion* as a powerful and compelling emotion or a strong feeling or experience of love.[13] But surprisingly, the first definition for *passion* in Webster's dictionary is "the sufferings of Christ between the night of the Last Supper and his death."[14]

Even Mr. Webster heard Jesus's melody line. Jesus's passion connects so clearly with us that it shapes the way we understand the word itself.

Jesus's cross was merely a means to a much bigger end. His cross signified a step in the process. He didn't cherish the cross itself, but what waited beyond the cross.

The author of Hebrews urges us to consider the way Jesus approached his cross so we will not grow weary and lose heart when carrying our own. We are told not to focus on our cross, but rather upon Jesus as our example.

> Let us fix our eyes on Jesus, the author and perfecter of our faith, who for the joy set before him endured the cross, scorning its shame, and sat down at the right hand of the throne of God. Consider him who endured such opposition from sinful men, so that you will not grow weary and lose heart."

Jesus embodies an idea much bigger than a religion. He transcended life and even politics, modeling a lesson applicable to every one of us. He embraced something every human faces—pain.

———◦◦◦◦◦———

So what about you? And what about your cross? More importantly, what about your crown?

Go ahead and ask someone about their cross. Or if that word doesn't connect, call it their "trial" or "pain point." Just inquire into who or what is bugging them. Most likely they'll give you a detailed speech with sub-points and illustrations about all the struggles in their lives. They are acquainted with the unique nuances of their cross.

However, ask these same people about their crown. Chances are that when you do, you'll get a puzzled look. Most people are foggy about it at best. And when we're foggy about our crown, then the weight of our cross will soon crush us. Clarity when considering our crown gives us courage when carrying our cross. One flows from the other.

American businessman and author Max De Pree says, "The first responsibility of a leader is to define reality."[15]

You might not accept the fact that you're a leader, or maybe you've never even considered yourself one. But the truth is you're leading your own life, whether your performance is stellar or poor. Responsibility for leading our lives can't be placed on the government, the economy, our business, our friends, our families, or our boss—if we have one.

If you want "the little difference" to emerge within your own life, then you need to question your condition. You have to be willing to turn down the noise and listen for the melody line emerging from your soul.

When you do, like Gabby, you'll find your voice.

And people want to hear it. Because when you have the courage to sing, you allow courage to do what all courage is meant to do: inspire others.

And we are a world in desperate need of inspiration.

PART
TWO
Feel—The How

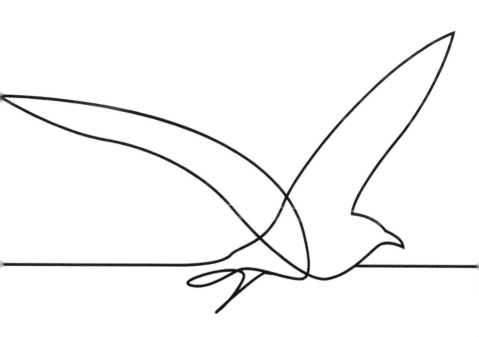

5

STEP ONE:
QUESTION YOUR CONDITION

*It's the question that drives us . . . it's the
question that brought you here.*

—Trinity, *The Matrix*

What annoys you?
Fingernails scratching on the chalkboard? Soup
served cold when you're starving? Important phone
calls dropped?

Did I get your number yet?

Maybe for you, it's not one of these but rather an empty
toilet paper roll when you're in desperate need of some? Or
the feeling you get when someone just stole your parking spot
and you're running late?

Do any of these raise your stress level?

For me, none of these compare to my biggest stressor:
being stuck. I hate being stuck, because stuck stinks! It's a
slow death by chronic pain.

I hate seeing other people stuck too. Someone wise correctly observed that the only difference between being stuck in a rut and stuck in a grave is six feet.

I don't think any of us choose to be stuck—we slip into it unintentionally. Given a little time, though, we become full-fledged residents. This doesn't excuse our condition. It only explains it.

Psychologists explain it further through something called "the four stages of competence" learning model. These stages are:

1. Unconscious Incompetence

2. Conscious Incompetence

3. Conscious Competence

4. Unconscious Competence

Here's how it works. Everyone starts at a place of unconscious incompetence. We don't know what we don't know, because we're ignorant. Eventually, some of us move to a place where we know what we don't know, a place of conscious incompetence. At this stage, at least we have a choice.

But many of us choose incorrectly.

We remain incompetent for fear of the unknown. We reason that with incompetence we're in control. Releasing control would mean bumping into conscious competence, but we fear letting go and focus more on what we might lose than what we might gain.

A few break free and stumble into a land of learning where everything is new and unfamiliar. Sure, mistakes arise, but so do our levels of competence. Given enough time, those of us who become consciously competent, if we remain on the path of transformation, will eventually move to a place of unconscious competence and master the skills we once didn't even know we were ignorant of.

To better understand, try on this example.

At one period in your life, you didn't know how to drive a car. When you were young, you didn't know that you didn't know. You simply sat in cars as a passenger, completely clueless that someday you might drive one. Like me, you were young, ignorant, and comfortable.

But time marched on.

I grew up, and so did my friends. One day, my friend's older brother mentioned getting his temporary license. I slowly became conscious of my incompetence. I knew I didn't know how to drive a car, but that day I vowed that one day I would. I made it my goal to move from conscious incompetence to conscious competence.

I began to study for my temporary license and to watch how other people drove. I listened to their reactions, and I observed their habits. Eventually, I took a driver's education class and sat behind the wheel for the first time. I moved from being stuck to unstuck.

Over time, I mastered the skill of driving.

At last, I arrived at the place I currently reside—a learned model of unconscious competence. I now occasionally drive entire trips across town without even consciously thinking about it. My eyes move from rearview mirror to driver's side mirror, and my hands remain in their proper position. I can even engage in a conversation with passengers or on my cell phone via a hands-free device.

My mind, my emotions, my body, and my spirit all unite in a time and space and operate with intelligence in an unconscious effort to achieve one particular goal. Not only do I benefit, but the passengers with me do as well. We all arrive safely at our intended destination.

As humans, our natural progression flows from unconscious

incompetence to conscious incompetence to conscious competence to unconscious competence.

Or for the visual learners, picture this:

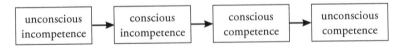

Although a learning model like this packs endless potential, the real key lies in moving from level 1 to level 2, or from ignorance to choice. When we're aware we're stuck, then we have options. We can stay there, and many do, or we can take The Deeper Path and move toward becoming unstuck.

When we lack the self-awareness we're stuck, it's highly unlikely we'll ever become unstuck. Just try to help an ignorant stuck person—you'll often get a large helping of anger and misunderstanding, such as in these three examples.

ONE: CONSIDER PHYSICAL HEALTH

Imagine suffering from abnormal weight loss and stomach pains. Now imagine someone telling you that you can't eat any gluten. Look at food labels sometime. Gluten finds its way into a whole bunch of items like wheat (including kamut and spelt), barley, rye, malts, and triticale.

The average person wouldn't eliminate gluten from their diet because someone told them to. But imagine if a doctor, through a series of testing, diagnosed you with celiac disease. Now imagine you saw the test results.

Because you moved from unconscious incompetence to conscious competence, from ignorance to accountability, you now have a choice. If you ignore the test results, you will have to pay up. According to Celiac.com, if someone with this disease continues to eat gluten, studies have shown that he or she will increase their chances of gastrointestinal cancer by a factor of 40 to 100 times.

Self-awareness comes at a cost. But ignorance does too.

STEP ONE: QUESTION YOUR CONDITION

Two: Consider Parenting

It's a whole lot easier giving your kid help when they realize they need it. And it's even better when they ask for help. But what if that same kid never realizes they need help? What then?

Can they ever be helped?

Not very easily.

What if you and I resemble that kid in more ways than we think?

How would we know? What if there are certain areas in our lives where we don't know what we don't know? What if we don't realize we're stuck?

How can we escape our unconscious incompetence and gain the self-awareness needed to see ourselves clearly?

Three: Consider Movies

Agent Smith unwrapped this phenomenon further in the movie *The Matrix*. He commented on the complexity of the Matrix. "Have you ever stood and stared at it, marveled at its beauty, its genius?" he said. "Billions of people just living out their lives, oblivious."[1]

In the film, the unconscious incompetence of humans gave sentient machines their edge. These machines depended on humanity's ignorance of their condition. These machines pacified the population with electrical impulses meant to distract them from the real truth: that they're stuck, serving the machines unknowingly.

Unfortunately, when we don't know what we don't know, why would we ever change? When we lack the self-awareness that another way even exists, how could we choose another option?

Morpheus understood this point and expounded to his protégé Neo:

The Matrix is a system, Neo. That system is our enemy. But when you're inside, you look around, what do you see? Businessmen, teachers, lawyers, carpenters. The very minds of the people we are trying to save. But until we do, these people are still a part of that system, and that makes them our enemy. You have to understand, most of these people are not ready to be unplugged. And many of them are so inured, so hopelessly dependent on the system, that they will fight to protect it."[2]

Sound familiar?

Sounds to me like the same kid who needs help but doesn't know he needs help. Sounds to me like the kid who sees her parent as the enemy, not the ally. Sounds like someone who's stuck but doesn't know it.

Morpheus continued to explain the gravity of the situation. "Have you ever had a dream, Neo, that you were so sure it was real? What if you were unable to awake from that dream? How would you know the difference between the dream world and the real world?"[3]

Morpheus warned Neo that ignorance isolated and insulated people from their ability to see themselves objectively. Those of us who know the storyline of the film know that Neo faced a choice: Would he risk his life to save the same people who longed both to kill him and to save the very system that enslaved them?

So how can we get unstuck if we're not aware we are stuck?

If we pay closer attention to the words we use, our vocabulary might just give us away.

Here's why.

We tend to use linguistic metaphors to explain the way we see ourselves. When we feel "up," we use phrases like:

I am on top of the world.	I am invincible.
I am unstoppable.	I am on a roll.
I am bulletproof.	I am on fire.

But we use other phrases when we feel stuck. We say things like:

I am missing a piece of the puzzle.   I am going in circles.
I am in the wrong frame of mind.   I can't snap out of it.
I need to think outside the box.   I am stuck in a rut.

These last six metaphors express a low level of awareness that we are stuck and powerless.

First we think it.

Then we feel it.

Then we say it.

And then we live into it and from it.

The cost of living from those phrases will take a toll on you and those around you. When swimming in this type of headspace, we often devote our awareness to our problems and end up losing touch with our own resourcefulness. In America alone much of the population feels stuck, held back, and detached from their own resourcefulness:

1. One-third of Americans are struggling to live to their "fullest potential."

2. Nearly seventy million Americans are dealing with emotional conflict.

3. Seventy million Americans feel held back by their past.[4]

French-born American author Anaïs Nin wrote, "We don't see things the way they are, we see things the way we are."[5] We're an extension of our world. When we're off-center, perplexed, or conflicted, then our world is as well.

We question our own power and ability to create and grow. We operate out of scarcity instead of abundance and become takers instead of givers. We only see what we're not and we

49

often become angry and frustrated. We crack open the door and let fear creep in. But thankfully, if we're self-aware, we also recognize a longing.

We become aware of a brighter future and a better possibility. Something in us awakens. We want to create a life that truly resembles what we believe is possible. We don't want to stay stuck anymore.

We want to grow. Our spirit, the most powerful part of us, speaks to us. Our spirit—the space where we give and receive signals to and from God—reveals a greater reality.

We feel called to a higher expression and a fuller expansion of our current awareness and achievement. Our spirit speaks to our soul through our discontentment and longing. And although these emotions might seem like uninvited guests, we should welcome them.

Remember—dead people feel nothing. No discontentment or longing, but also no pleasure or joy. Nothing.

Celebrate the reality that you feel something, even if it is unpleasant at the moment.

The fact that you feel is proof you're alive.

Saint Augustine wisely exhorted, "If you would attain to what you are not yet, you must always be displeased by what you are. For where you are pleased with yourself there you have remained. Keep adding, keep walking, keep advancing."[6]

Although his quote brings encouragement, it also brings admonishment. To feel the full weight of our potential, we first need to feel the full weight of our pain.

And to do this, we have only one option.

We must first unmask our painkillers.

6

STEP TWO:
UNMASK YOUR PAINKILLERS

We'll try and ease the pain, but somehow we all feel the same.

—Smashing Pumpkins

"**I** bring you the gift of these four words: I believe in you."

Those life-giving words are attributed to Blaise Pascal.

The first time someone gave me these four words sincerely, from their heart, I was a young man in desperate need of belief. These words altered my life, gave me wings, and changed the trajectory of my future.

Strangely, we're the last person to see our own potential. I'm confident that, at this exact moment, you don't see your full potential. But I do. Grant me the privilege of possibly being the first person ever to express the truth: I believe in you. And I want you to achieve all that you've been created for.

But for you to do so, I'm going to have to inject a little acute pain into this chapter. Call it tough love, but it's the only way I've grown and continue to grow.

I have a few truth-tellers in my life. I know they love me because they care more about my growth than my temporary happiness. Sometimes they're pretty direct with me. Other times they throw a challenge my way. Bottom line: they help me go faster and further. And so, I'd like to throw a little challenge your way.

I dare you to do something.

I bet you'll find it difficult because, like me, you've been hardwired and conditioned not to do it. Why, you may ask?

Well, that's a difficult question to answer. Maybe it's because we've been trained that it's wasteful or lazy. But those are probably just excuses. So let's dig a little deeper and take another step.

I think you're addicted. (I know I am.)

I'm not referring to an addiction to substances or sex. It's an addiction to something much subtler.

Noise. We all crave noise.

Hundreds of years ago Pascal saw this tendency, even before, TV or movies, electricity, or the internet. He wrote, "All of man's difficulties are caused by his inability to sit quietly in a room by himself."[1]

Maybe you're thinking, *Really? All of our difficulties are caused by a lack of reflection that results from an addiction to noise?*

I encourage you to take a shot at my dare. Go sixty seconds. Shut off everything you can. Your phone, your music, your TV. Whatever is on. If it has a switch, turn it off.

Why? What's the point? Here's the truth: If it's not that big of a deal, then do it. Take one minute and invest in your future. Take one minute to unmask your painkiller.

Sit still for sixty seconds. Hit pause, and close your eyes.

(Sixty-second pause.)

If you took the challenge, What did you think? What did you hear? What did you feel? Try to verbalize your experience. If you're exceptionally daring, journal your thoughts.

OK. Now that you're warmed up, let's step it up. Try five minutes. This may be tough, especially if you're addicted to productivity, but when was the last time you sat in silence for five minutes?

One day?

One week?

One year?

One life?

Try five minutes of silence. Hit pause and close your eyes. (Five-minute pause.)

Turning down the noise helps us to think better. And we all know that most people don't think. Thomas Edison said, "Five percent of the people think; ten percent of the people think they think; and the other eighty-five percent would rather die than think."[2]

Many people prefer to be amused instead. But consider the word *amusement* and its etymology for a moment.

A = not

Muse = think

Amusement = to not think

When we're amused, we're distracted and diverted. These distractions and diversions waste our time. Sadly, many people don't mind because they don't value their time.

M. Scott Peck reveals the real cost of that misunderstanding. He warns, "Until you value yourself, you won't value your time. Until you value your time, you won't do anything with it."

"UNTIL YOU VALUE YOURSELF, YOU WON'T VALUE YOUR TIME. UNTIL YOU VALUE YOUR TIME, YOU WON'T DO ANYTHING WITH IT."

Noise numbs us to the deeper questions of life. And unfortunately, noise comes in many forms, including relationships with others. For example, why do we default to others when we need advice? Why do we seek out their noise before we even consider an answer for ourselves? Many of us are addicted to other people's opinions. The late Steve Jobs warned us about this tendency:

> *Your time is limited, so don't waste it living someone else's life. Don't be trapped by dogma—which is living with the results of other people's thinking. Don't let the noise of others' opinions drown out your own inner voice.*[3]

Counselors, coaches, teachers, pastors, trainers, friends, and family can all contribute their experience and insight into our situation, but at the end of the day, we're responsible for the action (or inaction) we choose.

Noise only contributes to the fog if we don't first take the time to be silent.

This internal work must be done before our defining moment arrives. Remember our friend Captain Sully? He did his hard work before the bird strike. When opportunity unveiled itself, he could act immediately because his mind was clear.

Bono recognizes this, and believes the common thread between great leaders is their "ability to see through the din and clangor of ideas and conversations and points of view, and hear the melody line, and realize: this is the thing we've got to do, this is more important than the others."[4]

Noise will come. It's inevitable. But if we do our soul surgery before the crisis, then when the choice comes we will be ready. When we prepare for the moment, the moment is prepared for us.

7

STEP THREE:
EXPLORE YOUR WOUNDS

*It is impossible for a man to learn what he
thinks he already knows.*

—Epictetus

"What do you want?"
A friend of mine asked me this many
years back, and the question ripped through
my routine.

He pressed further when I couldn't articulate my desire.
"What do you really want?"

I delayed, but he wouldn't let me go.

"Do you even know what you really want?"

By now, you might be able to tell I invite some very "direct"
people into my life. I even pay some of them to coach me
because I'm that committed to reaching my potential.

But I didn't always invite accountability—quite the opposite. At one point in my life, I avoided it altogether. I camped
out in my comfort zone. It took a while, but I eventually

learned firsthand that all growth happens outside of our comfort zone.

This is true in every area of our lives—physically, emotionally, spiritually, and even financially. I'll use money to illustrate the point because we all understand its value.

Imagine your annual income. If you don't have one, just pick a number.

Now imagine that being your monthly income. Would you like that to be true?

Most people would enjoy such an arrangement. But these same people, if you asked them to sit down with you and create a plan to achieve this, would begin to argue why it's an impossibility.

"You don't understand: I don't have the necessary degree, training, or skills."
"You don't understand: my situation is different."
"You don't understand: I'm from a small town."
"You don't understand: I can't do that."

Simply put, most people argue for what they don't want.

Remember those universal laws we discussed earlier, such as gravity? Time to meet another one: the Law of Argument: *We get what we argue for.*

Most of us say we want more money, but then we'd argue why it can't be a reality for us.

Change the circumstances, and the law still works. Ask a heroin addict if she wants to be free. Odds are she'll say yes. Then, when you try to create a plan, she'll argue why it won't work for her.

"You don't understand: all my friends are heroin addicts too."
"You don't understand: I've never made it a day without it."
"You don't understand: my dealer is my neighbor."
"You don't understand: I need it."

I have a personal policy when I coach people: I never make an agreement with their unbelief. I don't let them off the hook or allow them to hide behind their excuses. This is because I care about them and their potential way too much.

Here's the sad truth: most of us self-sabotage. We don't need to worry about our competition, because we're already set on defeating ourselves. We can even see unbelief in our word choices. When considering our dreams, we quit before we get started. We give ourselves an out.

How much energy will it require?
How much will it cost?
How long will it take?

These phrases already admit defeat and open the door for escape.

Consider a crude example from the life of conquistador Hernando Cortez. Legend has it that before he came to the New World, he discussed with his men the potential treasure that resided within the new land. He told them how the treasure could enrich their lives and provide for their children's children.

But when they finally landed on the shore, his men lacked motivation and commitment. They reflected upon those who had made attempts in the past and failed. So Cortez did something unexpected.

He burned their ships.

He eliminated their ability to escape.

He erased their excuses.

Cortez didn't make an agreement with their unbelief.

We might not be exploring new lands today, but most of us are facing a similar challenge. We desire expansion. We want to be more, do more, have more, and give more than we currently experience. But we won't achieve this with *average*.

Nobody wants average, whether it's food, entertainment, or an experience. We pay for excellence. We want exceptional.

And although we expect it from others, we often believe it's impossible for ourselves.

> WE DON'T GET WHAT WE WANT; WE GET WHO WE ARE.

We don't get what we want; we get who we are. We're the lid on our own potential, and we can never outperform our own self-image.

———⦵⦵⦵———

So how do we get off the proverbial dime?

Movement starts by first understanding where we stand. Unfortunately, instead of standing in God's truth, too often we stand in the circle of our own truth.

This is the circle of what we believe is possible for us.

This is the circle known as our comfort zone.

This is the circle of our own awareness.

Within this circle, we try to convince ourselves that we're content with being content and satisfied with satisfactory.

But we're not.

And when we're not growing and creating the life we know we're meant to experience, our spirit stirs. We use words to describe the place we're at, the place of our discontentment. We conceive something better, but we're not sure how to get there.

We see "stuck" wherever we go. But every so often we let our mind drift to what could be. We daydream because dreams are free. We fail to realize that dreams are found on a tollway, not a highway. They come with a cost. And unfortunately, we don't pay just once. We pay daily.

Some of us see this cost and crumble. But the price really doesn't matter. The price can be high or low. As long as it's more than we have, we stagger under the weight. We see the gap, take inventory of what we don't have, and become discouraged at the apparent distance we need to travel.

We falter because we think we don't have what it takes, and we sink into a shortage of self-belief. Unfortunately, we don't see value in ourselves, and as a result, we don't invest in ourselves. Instead, we wait for a sponsor. Even though we lack belief in ourselves, we want others to believe in us.

We fail to understand the Law of Belief: *Before others choose to believe in you, they naturally judge if you believe in yourself.*

We taste our self-limiting beliefs and we sense the void between what is and what could be. This distance is defined as the "gap of intention," or some experts label it as the "intention-behavior gap."[1] In simpler terms, it's the disconnection between knowing and doing.

Morpheus illustrates this gap when he tells Neo, "Stop trying to hit me and hit me!"[1] Although Neo wanted to hit Morpheus, for some reason he couldn't. An obvious gap existed.

In the book of Mark, we see this gap in the dialogue between the father of a demon-possessed boy and Jesus. After Jesus asks him if he's willing to exercise faith, he tells the rabbi, "I do believe, help my unbelief." Although he had faith that Jesus could heal people, for some reason he didn't think Jesus could heal his son.

In our own physical health, there are also gaps between our knowing and our doing. We're aware of steps we could take to ensure better physical health, whether it be more exercise, better eating habits, or longer sleeping patterns. But many of us never do these things.

The solution to this gap isn't more knowledge. The gap between knowing and doing is always bridged with being. We're human *beings*, not human *doings*. What we do is always an extension of who we are, not what we know.

Our natural response is often fear. We fear our own ability to bridge the gap. We fear failure and exposure. We fear leaving our comfort zone. We suffer from self-judgment, and we worry what the neighbors will think.

But here's a little secret: the neighbors don't think.

We sit paralyzed with fear about other people's impressions, but they're too caught up in their own story to even care.

The most critical jury resides inside our own minds, not within other people. And the people around us, the ones we're so afraid of, they're looking to us as an example. They're just as scared, and they're in desperate need of a bold model.

Hence one of the reasons movies are so popular. We enjoy watching other people overcome their own obstacles so we can have courage when facing ours. Unfortunately, we often use the same approach when it comes to our own lives as we do when watching movies. We're spectators in our own lives, accepting our lives rather than leading them.

Although we create a mental model of perfection for our lives, we can't step into it. Although we believe in a better way and a better world, we can't live from it. Although we aspire and long to change, we find ourselves stuck.

And so we do what we were taught to do: we begin to blame. We blame those around us and the circumstances of our life.

We blame our significant other.	We blame the politicians.
We blame our employees.	We blame our bosses.
We blame the economy.	We blame the markets.

And we remain bound to the circumstances and conditions of our lives, never realizing that the content of our lives does not need to create a prison.

If we could only get outside ourselves long enough to see the scenery, then we'd acknowledge this other way. To go higher, we must dig deeper.

Here's what I mean. Look beneath you right now. There's carpet, grass, tile, floor, sand, or air. Now, look around you. There are trees, buildings, or walls of some sort. Consider the walls. Have you ever realized what's behind them? Insulation? Drywall? Wood? Nails?

If you're sitting in a chair then consider: Do you feel your back against the chair? Do you feel your feet against the floor?

Certainly, there is more than we're aware of. And everything matters. Try to name one thing that doesn't matter.

Consider the little piece of plastic under certain table legs the next time you eat. Think it's unimportant? Try eating your dinner on a wobbly table and you'll quickly thank the designer of that little piece of plastic.

Or try to consider a world without staples the next time you present an important talk. Or one without paperclips, or pens, or personal computers.

I remember putting together one of my kid's Christmas toys one December evening. Toward the end of the project, I realized I was missing one small screw. The whole toy fell apart because of an insignificant little piece.

Was that screw really insignificant? Are you really insignificant?

There are only two types of people, and you're either one or the other. There's no third option. The truth is, we live with the mindset of either a victim or a victor. This choice kind of cuts out the middle ground, doesn't it?

So, which "map of the world" do you ascribe to? A victim believes the world happens to them. A victor believes they happen to the world. Either we blame people for our lack, or we take responsibility for what we don't yet possess. Our choice affects the way we see ourselves and the way we see the world around us. It's the frequency we give off to others, and it's the reason we attract some people and repel others. Who we choose to be is who we will become.

When we live from this victim mindset, we find fulfillment in adding to the drama by surrounding ourselves with people who agree with the story inside our head. We have the same conversations that strengthen our version of the truth. Our favorite songs confirm the injustice, and our favorite films add color and richness to our interpretation of correctness.

What if you had more power than you've ever imagined? What if you could peek past your pain and into your potential? What if you saw yourself as the victor you were created to be?

Your breakthrough moment begins when you drop the excuses.

8

FOUR:
O   YOUR EXCUSES

*or making excuses is seldom
for anything else.*

enjamin Franklin

I   ┠.
          er six thousand years of recorded his-
          man, woman, or child had ever done the
im   ..til that day, all of humanity bought into a
pai   .-limiting belief—except for a select few. That's
why so many people showed up to see if he could do it. Not
only did the general public believe such a feat was impossible,
but many doctors also weighed in, proclaiming that it was
lethal.

Run a mile in under four minutes and you will die. That's
pretty thick adversity. That's a prediction that could produce
some excellent excuses. Unless, of course, you didn't buy into
that self-limiting belief.

No wonder a crowd showed up at Iffley Road Track in Oxford that day. They were guaranteed a spectacle, no matter how you sliced it.

Until this time, the best humanity could dish out was a time of 4 minutes and 1.3 seconds, run by Gunder Hagg of Sweden in 1945. A barrier obviously existed, but few recognized it for what it was: a barrier of belief.

Although a psychological mystique hung heavy around the four-minute barrier, several runners in the early 1950s dedicated themselves to being the first to break it. A noble goal—these runners didn't know if they were chasing their death sentence as well. The doctors seemed to think so.

A six-foot-one medical student, Roger Bannister not only believed the impossible was possible, but also that he would be the one to do it. Obstacles were no stranger to Bannister. His parents couldn't afford to send him to school, so he ran his way to admission by winning a track scholarship to Oxford, where he studied medicine and evolved into a running sensation.

Not everything went Roger's way though. He also suffered from self-limiting beliefs. The 1952 Olympics weren't kind to him. After failing dismally with a fourth-place finish, Bannister spent two months deciding whether to give up running altogether.

He decided to keep going and intensified his training. Roger did hard interval running with the two-year-old memory of disappointment still burning within him. Although he had fallen short in the past, each day he trained he took one step closer to his goal. Bannister believed the man who could drive himself further once the effort got painful would be the man who would win. And so, he pushed hard, especially when the pain set in.

Reporters recorded their observations, and their perspective is just as fresh today as when it was penned over fifty years ago. The AP reported:

Bannister bided his time until about 300 yards from the tape when he urged himself to a supreme effort. With a machine-like, seemingly effortless stride he drew away steadily from Chataway and, head thrown back slightly, he breasted the cool, stiff wind on the last turn to come driving down the homestretch to climax his spectacular performance.[1]

Although this is an insightful report, Bannister provided us with a better, below the surface, perspective: "No longer conscious of my movement, I discovered a new unity with nature. I had found a new source of power and beauty, a source I never dreamt existed."

He crossed the finish line and collapsed to the ground, drained of energy. "It was only then that real pain overtook me," he said. "I felt like an exploded flashlight with no will to live; I just went on existing in the most passive physical state without being unconscious."[2]

The crowd let loose when the announcer uttered Bannister's time, not even allowing him the privilege of finishing his sentence. All they needed to hear was three minutes and then applause overtook the rest of the announcement: 59.4 seconds.

Looking back now, it's obvious that breaking the four-minute mile was more of a psychological feat than a physical one. Bannister broke a belief first and a record second. Insiders understood that the new record resulted from a new belief. Volumes could be written about the events that transpired shortly after.

Within forty-six days of Bannister's breakthrough, John Landy in Finland surpassed the record with a time of 3:57.9. Many runners followed after.

By the end of 1957, sixteen runners had logged sub-four-minute miles. And in the last fifty years, the mile record has been lowered by almost seventeen seconds, an eternity in the running world. Currently, the mile record is held by Morocco's Hicham El Guerrouj, who ran a time of 3:43.13 in Rome in 1999.

Clearly, the four-minute mile barrier resided only in the minds of individuals. Roger Bannister broke that belief, and runners have been breaking the record ever since.

⸻⸻ ◦◦◦ ⸻⸻

What self-limiting beliefs swim around in your brain?

Self-limiting beliefs are nothing new. They've been hijacking human hearts and sabotaging human potential since the beginning. Fear tricks our minds into obeying illogical commands and submitting to unfounded statements. Our subconscious can't easily discern between reality and fantasy. This is why rationalizing with a three-year-old about the pretend monster under the bed doesn't pay big dividends.

> SELF-LIMITING BELIEFS ARE NOTHING NEW. THEY'VE BEEN HIJACKING HUMAN HEARTS AND SABOTAGING HUMAN POTENTIAL SINCE THE BEGINNING.

We rarely see how self-limiting beliefs prevent potential and hinder healing when it comes to our own lives. Yet if we frame self-limiting beliefs within the backdrop of inventions and technologies, we quickly see the futility and fallacy of such thinking. Thankfully, a few courageous pioneers overcame the excuses that defined the popular thinking of their day. Here are a few famous ones:

There is no reason anyone would want a computer in their home. Ken Olson, president, chairman, and founder of Digital Equipment Corp. (DEC), maker of big business mainframe computers, arguing against the PC, 1977

So we went to Atari and said, "Hey, we've got this amazing thing, even built with some of your parts, and what do you think about funding us? Or we'll give it to you. We just want to do it. Pay our salary, we'll come work for you." And they said, *"No."* So then we went to Hewlett-Packard, and they said, *"Hey, we don't need you. You haven't got through college yet."*

Steve Jobs, founder of Apple Computer, Inc., on his and Steve Wozniak's early attempts to distribute their personal computer.

It will be years—not in my time—before a woman will become prime minister.

Margaret Thatcher, future prime minister, October 26, 1969

With over fifteen types of foreign cars already on sale here, the Japanese auto industry isn't likely to carve out a big share of the market for itself.

BusinessWeek, August 2, 1968

Remote shopping, while entirely feasible, will flop—because women like to get out of the house, like to handle merchandise, like to be able to change their minds.

Newsweek, predicting popular holidays for the late 1960s

There is practically no chance communications space satellites will be used to provide better telephone, telegraph, television, or radio service inside the United States.

T. Craven, FCC Commissioner, 1961 (the first commercial communications satellite went into service in 1965)

We don't like their sound, and guitar music is on the way out.
Decca Records, when they rejected The Beatles, 1962

The world potential market for copying machines is 5,000 at most.

> IBM, to the eventual founders of Xerox,
> saying the photocopier had no market large
> enough to justify production, 1959

To place a man in a multi-stage rocket and project him into the controlling gravitational field of the moon where the passengers can make scientific observations, perhaps land alive, and then return to earth—all that constitutes a wild dream worthy of Jules Verne. I am bold enough to say that such a man-made voyage will never occur regardless of all future advances.

> Lee DeForest, American radio pioneer and
> inventor of the vacuum tube, 1957

Television won't last. It's a flash in the pan.

> Mary Somerville, pioneer of radio
> educational broadcasts, 1948

There is not the slightest indication that nuclear energy will ever be obtainable. It would mean that the atom would have to be shattered at will.

> Albert Einstein, 1932

The wireless music box has no imaginable commercial value. Who would pay for a message sent to no one in particular?

> Associates of David Sarnoff responding to the
> latter's call for investment in the radio, 1921

Taking the best left-handed pitcher in baseball and converting him into a right fielder is one of the dumbest things I ever heard.

> Tris Speaker, baseball expert, talking
> about Babe Ruth, 1919

STEP FOUR: OVERCOME YOUR EXCUSES

The cinema is little more than a fad. It's canned drama. What audiences really want to see is flesh and blood on the stage.
> Charlie Chaplin, actor, producer, director,
> and studio founder, 1916

The idea that cavalry will be replaced by these iron coaches is absurd. It is little short of treasonous.
> Comment of an aide-de-camp to Field Marshal
> Haig, at tank demonstration, 1916

There will never be a bigger plane built.
> A Boeing engineer, after the first flight of the 247,
> a twin-engine plane that holds ten people.

Sensible and responsible women do not want to vote.
> Grover Cleveland, US president, 1905

Airplanes are interesting toys but of no military value.
> Marshal Ferdinand Foch, professor of strategy, 1904

The horse is here to stay, but the automobile is only a novelty— a fad.
> The president of the Michigan Savings Bank
> advising Henry Ford's lawyer, Horace Rackham,
> not to invest in the Ford Motor Co., 1903

Man will not fly for fifty years.
> Wilbur Wright, American aviation pioneer, to brother
> Orville, after a disappointing flying experiment, 1901
> (their first successful flight was in 1903)

I must confess that my imagination refuses to see any sort of submarine doing anything but suffocating its crew and floundering at sea.
> H. G. Wells, British novelist, 1901

It doesn't matter what he does, he will never amount to anything.
> Albert Einstein's teacher to his father, 1895

Fooling around with alternating current is just a waste of time. Nobody will use it, ever.
> Thomas Edison, American inventor, 1889

We are probably nearing the limit of all we can know about astronomy.
> Simon Newcomb, Canadian-born
> American astronomer, 1888

This "telephone" has too many shortcomings to be seriously considered as a means of communication. The device is inherently of no value to us.
> A memo at Western Union, 1878

When the Paris Exhibition [of 1878] closes, electric light will close with it and no more will be heard of it.
> Oxford professor Erasmus Wilson

The abdomen, the chest, and the brain will forever be shut from the intrusion of the wise and humane surgeon.
> John Eric Ericksen, British surgeon, appointed
> Surgeon Extraordinary to Queen Victoria, 1873

No one will pay good money to get from Berlin to Potsdam in one hour when he can ride his horse there in one day for free.
> King William I of Prussia, on hearing of
> the invention of trains, 1864

They couldn't hit an elephant at this dist—
> Last words of Gen. John Sedgwick, spoken as
> he looked out over the parapet at enemy lines during
> the Battle of Spotsylvania Court House, 1864

Drill for oil? You mean drill into the ground to try and find oil? You're crazy.

> Associates of Edwin L. Drake refusing his
> suggestion to drill for oil, 1859

The abolishment of pain in surgery is a chimera. It is absurd to go on seeking it . . . knife and pain are two words in surgery that must forever be associated in the consciousness of the patient.

> Dr. Alfred Velpeau, French surgeon, 1839

Rail travel at high speed is not possible because passengers, unable to breathe, would die of asphyxia.

> Dr. Dionysys Larder, professor of natural philosophy
> and astronomy, University College London, 1830

So many centuries after the Creation it is unlikely that anyone could find hitherto unknown lands of any value.

> Committee advising King Ferdinand and
> Queen Isabella of Spain regarding a proposal
> by Christopher Columbus, 1486

A quick survey reveals that self-limiting beliefs intrude into every facet and fabric of our lives, including:

Entertainment	Literature	Sports
Government	Air travel	Phone
Land travel	Electricity	Music
Technology	Business	Radio
Exploration	Shipping	Film
Astronomy	Medicine	Law
Commerce	Science	War
Computers	Culture	TV
Sea travel	Energy	
Weaponry	Health	

Look around you for a moment. Nearly everything I see (toys, food, electric light, carpet, shoes, clocks, candy, heating blankets, remotes, reclining furniture, books, cardboard) once encountered self-limiting beliefs.

At one point, none of them existed. Humanity needed to overcome the excuses that limited the creation and production of such ideas. Somewhere, sometime, someone felt the need to overcome the excuses. They exchanged popular thinking and conventional wisdom for a higher goal and loftier possibilities. They considered the cost (danger, ridicule, shame) and paid it for something more valuable: potential.

Don't forget, the Wright brothers didn't have a pilot's license. And the laws of flight have always existed. They certainly didn't create them. Rather, they overcame the excuses and put those laws to work.

So what about you and your context? What self-limiting beliefs are preventing your progress and ensuring your anonymity? Which of your ideas remain undeveloped? How are popular thinking and conventional wisdom restricting you?

If you want an excuse, you'll certainly find one. But what happens after you blow through one? Chances are you'll blow through another—and another. You'll always find more. Sure, there's pain in stepping out. But there's also pain in holding back.

I decided a long time ago to abandon a life of regret. I decided to embrace life, even if it includes failure. Failure means I'm moving. And being stuck stinks.

Maybe, up until this day, you've bought into a particular self-limiting belief. But today this can change. Instead of taking inventory of why you can't, begin to reframe your response. Start saying, "Up until now . . ."

Up until now, I was enslaved by past failures.

Up until now, I let fear hold me back.

Up until now, I wouldn't take action.

A barrier obviously exists, but this barrier of belief has sabotaged your success long enough. Although not everything has gone your way, you haven't given up. As Roger Bannister found out, the people who drive themselves further once it gets painful are the people who will win.

9

STEP FIVE:
EMBODY YOUR HEALING

*You cannot kindle a fire in any other heart
until it is burning within your own.*

—Eleanor Doan

Remember Simon Cowell?

Years ago, if you found yourself standing in line to audition for a certain talent show and heard the name "Simon Cowell," most likely one specific feeling swept through your soul.

Fear.

As a talent judge on *American Idol*, Simon Cowell made sure to live up to his infamous reputation. Besides his verbal jabs and no-nonsense style, he'd start the judging process by asking each contestant the same penetrating question.

With a net worth of over 320 million dollars and an annual salary of 75 million, his one question could be literally categorized as "the million-dollar question."[1]

At the height of each season, as he and the other judges observed hundreds of auditions daily, he rarely changed his opening question. For some reason, it defined him as much as the brutal insults he so willingly doled out.

No matter how you feel about Simon, you can't argue with his intuition.

His track record proves he could sniff out superstars like Kelly Clarkson and Carrie Underwood. And his expertise enabled him to identify less than favorable acts as well. He cut through the fog of talent (or lack thereof) and extracted the elite, crowning rock star royalty without a second thought.

All because of one single question.

Before contestants gave their background, said their name, or sang a note, one single question confronted confidence and unlocked their story.

He didn't ask, "What do your friends think of your voice?" or "How long have you been singing?" or "Are you in a band?"

Nope. None of these sufficed.

Instead, the one question Simon asked more than any other was, "What makes you think you're the next American Idol?"

That's it. And the correct answer converted into millions of dollars of potential revenue. Most contestants gave a variety of replies:

"Because I've won awards for my singing."

"Because I've been doing this all my life."

"Because I have a vocal coach."

But none of these answers caught Simon's attention. Only one answer predicted potential in this multimillionaire's mind. And only one answer will predict your potential.

You've made it to Step Five. You've come a long way so far. We've addressed the Why of The Deeper Path and most of the How. But we still have one more section to go: the What.

If you've encountered some fear along the way, you're not alone. Everyone who takes The Deeper Path does. But this is what sets you apart from others. You've kept going. In the words of Cus D'Amato, "The hero and the coward both feel exactly the same fear, only the hero confronts his fear and converts it to fire."[2]

At this last Step, we must confront our fears—and in the process, we'll find our courage. I've discovered that although I can never silence my fears, I can put them in proper perspective. Instead of letting them occupy the main stage in my life, I've been able to turn down their volume. Now these voices are barely audible, background music at best. Because of this adjustment, I've been able to discover my voice and sing my melody line.

We can only accomplish this by excavating our fears and confronting them one at a time. So get your shovel and let's start digging into the Big Three:

1. Fear of Change

2. Fear of Failure

3. Fear of Success

FEAR OF CHANGE

As children, we needed change just to survive. If not, we'd still be in diapers, drinking out of baby bottles, and wearing bibs.

As adults, we look at change differently—almost unfavorably. We evolve into creatures of habit. We prefer what we know because it's safer. We stop playing to win, and instead we start playing not to lose. We ignore Eric Hoffer's warning: "People will cling to an unsatisfactory way of life rather than change to get something better for fear of getting something worse."[3]

We crave routine because we crave control. Giving up control requires a death of sorts. French writer Anatole France said, "All changes, even the most longed for, have their melancholy; for what we leave behind is part of ourselves; we

WE CRAVE ROUTINE BECAUSE WE CRAVE CONTROL.

must die to one life before we can enter into another."[4]

No wonder change is scary. To change is to die and then be reborn. This cycle produces growth, but it also produces pain. I experience this every time I get a phone upgrade. For the first few days, I hate my new phone. Even though I know the new technology will help me go further faster, I can't stand the learning curve. But give it three days, and I love the new phone and never want to go back—until the next upgrade a couple years later.

Although this is a trivial example, it can be applied to more epic illustrations as well, such as the Law of Sacrifice. John Maxwell coined this Law by explaining, *we need to give up to go up.*[5]

We often misunderstand the Law of Sacrifice and redefine it as the Law of Tradeoff: *exchanging something of lesser value for something of greater value.* Unfortunately, this isn't the truth. Giving up means letting go *first*, without the guarantee of anything in exchange. It's an act of faith that contains a real risk. Charles DuBois referred to it as the ability "at any moment to sacrifice what we are for what we would become."[6]

The Deeper Path contains change at every corner. If we want to walk the path, then we must be willing to change. But remember—when we change, so do our relationships. This injects panic into people who are addicted to relationships. To continue on the path, we must break free. We still value relationships, but we don't derive our worth from them.

Because we're committed to growth and change, we might lose some friendships along the way. But know this: a friend who demands we stay the same isn't a true friend. Healthy friendships propel us forward. They don't hold us back.

Eric Hoffer warns us about the cost of not changing: "In times of change learners inherit the earth; while the learned find themselves beautifully equipped to deal with a world that no longer exists."[7]

Life is change. We can either invite it or ignore it. But realize that change will show up at the party with or without an invitation.

FEAR OF FAILURE

In my travels as a speaker, I met a man at one of my events who regretfully told me a story from thirty years prior. Evidently, back in high school, he sat in class one day with a blank notebook in front of him. The teacher asked him to work out a math problem on the chalkboard. He stood in front of the class for three minutes, unable to solve the problem. When he returned to his desk, he looked at his notebook, and someone had written FAILURE in capital letters across it.

He told me, "For the next thirty years, that name shaped my life. Every day I ran from the label FAILURE. It held me back and prevented me from taking risks in business and love."

As tragic as this story sounds, I know fear of failure shapes many of us. Looking at the way people live, it's like they believe in reincarnation—they're waiting for the next life to come alive.

Bestselling author Rick Warren identifies three types of people: "There are those who make things happen, those who watch things happen & those who have no idea what's happening."[8]

Which one are you? Few of us fall into the first category. We let fear prevent us from even trying.

Others of us suffer from analysis paralysis. We study things to death before stepping into action. John Henry Newman warned, "A man would do nothing if he waited until he could do it so well that no one could find fault."[9]

The truth is, we will fail. It's part of life. But be encouraged: fear means we're moving, growing, and exploring. The alternative is never trying, a clear indication we're already dead.

Certain business cultures demand their employees fail a certain amount of the time, as long as they're attempting new things. They view failure positively because it means they're expanding beyond comfort zones.

Theodore Roosevelt, a leader known for risk, adventure, and an entrepreneurial spirit, brought with him a unique perspective on failure:

> *It's not the critic who counts, not the one who points out how the strong man stumbled or how the doer of deeds might have done them better. The credit belongs to the man who is actually in the arena; whose face is marred with the sweat and dust and blood; who strives valiantly; who errs and comes up short again and again; who knows the great enthusiasms, the great devotions and spends himself in a worthy cause and who, at best knows the triumph of high achievement and who at worst, if he fails, at least fails while daring greatly so that his place shall never be with those cold and timid souls who know neither victory nor defeat.*[10]

FEAR OF SUCCESS

This last fear may sound strange at first, but I see it spring up in my coaching clients more and more. We're afraid of our own success.

Here's why.

Success is a type of magnifying glass. The spotlight shines brighter when you're on the stage. Most of us know our flaws, and we fear exposure. We do everything to hide those weaknesses. Standing on a bigger stage guarantees a higher level of scrutiny.

We rationalize that as long as we're in the crowd, at least we can wear our masks. We know our makeup can't cover up every imperfection, so we play small to maintain our image. We want a bigger stage—but not one big enough to reveal us.

We fail to understand that success means deep awareness of our failures. Our failures enable us to connect with others. They make us approachable and believable. The sooner we get comfortable with ourselves, the sooner others feel comfortable around us. In the proper context, sharing our failures often liberates others, allowing them to be more at peace with who they are.

I never tire of Marianne Williamson's famous words:

Our deepest fear is not that we are inadequate. Our deepest fear is that we are powerful beyond measure. It is our light, not our darkness that most frightens us. We ask ourselves, Who am I to be brilliant, gorgeous, talented, fabulous? Actually, who are you not to be? You are a child of God. Your playing small does not serve the world. There is nothing enlightened about shrinking so that other people won't feel insecure around you. We are all meant to shine, as children do. We were born to make manifest the glory of God that is within us. It's not just in some of us; it's in everyone. And as we let our own light shine, we unconsciously give other people permission to do the same. As we are liberated from our own fear, our presence automatically liberates others.[11]

Just for the sake of comparison, I flipped her thinking and rewrote the passage from the opposite angle. Sadly, this is a more accurate reflection of how most people think:

Our deepest fear is not that we are powerful. Our deepest fear is that we are inadequate beyond measure. It is our darkness, not our light, that most frightens us. We should ask ourselves, Who am I to be brilliant, gorgeous, talented, fabulous? Actually, you're right, who are you to be? You're not a child of God. Your playing big does not serve the world. There is something enlightening about shrinking so that other people won't feel insecure around you. We are not all meant to shine, as children do. We weren't born to make manifest the glory of God that is within us. In fact, it's only in some of us; not in everyone. And as we let our own darkness expand, we unconsciously give other people permission to do the same. As we are enslaved by our own fear, our presence automatically enslaves others.

Talk about a conversation killer! This version douses the fire and quenches the passion inside each one of us. And when you're not on fire, neither is your world. Sadly, this is the song many of us keep singing.

But it's time for you to sing a new song.

It's been said that many people are dead, but they just haven't made it official. The bulk of people die at twenty-five but are buried at seventy-five. I've seen too many real-life examples to think quips like this are funny.

Concentration camp survivor Viktor Frankl, a man who could have let fear consume him, understood the cost of fear: "Fear makes come true that which one is afraid of."[12]

Before we close out this chapter, you may want to know the correct answer Simon Cowell wanted to hear to his question, "What makes you think you're the next American Idol?"

The answer that predicted potential is the same answer your future tribe needs to hear from you. It sounds something like this:

Because this is who I was born to be.

Because this is my calling.

Because I already am.

His question served as a window into the contestants' hearts and souls. Simon wanted to see inside. Before he judged their voices, he actually judged their beliefs. Although fear and faith can coexist, one is always stronger. One will always win.

So which one is speaking louder inside of you? Faith or fear?

I'll tell you the same thing I tell my clients: Be the part before you get the part. Popular thinking might catch up with you someday, but then again, it might not. No worries. When you're this deep, their opinions don't matter anymore.

PART
THREE

Alive—The What

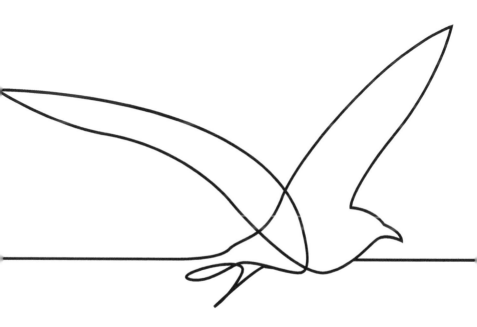

10

ONE HAPPY REUNION

This world is a great sculptor's workshop. We are the statues and there is a rumor going round the shop that some of us are some day going to come to life.

—C. S. Lewis

There were 155 people, including Captain Sully, hanging in thin air 3,000 feet over New York City.

They found themselves descending rapidly to the earth without any engine power.

These circumstances are enough to make any pilot wake up in the middle of the night, heart racing, drenched in a cold sweat. But this was the hand life dealt Captain Sullenberger that day. And he had only moments to make his next play.

Thirty seconds after the engines failed, he radioed air traffic control looking for a place to land. LaGuardia and Teterboro were both suggested, but as the plane fell rapidly so did the list of possible options.

Captain Sullenberger informed air traffic control of their inevitable destination: "We're going into the Hudson."

They were two and a half minutes into the flight and just one minute after the bird strike. This decision came with a cost, with passengers and crew watching it unfold, powerless.

One person acted.

I've seen a computer simulation of this infamous flight on YouTube.[1] Although the flight leaves the viewer in wonderment, what amazes me even more is Captain Sully's cool demeanor and ability to focus in spite of the noise produced by the co-pilot scrambling, the engines failing, the adrenaline pumping, and air traffic control interrupting.

If you listen closely to the dialogue, you'll know what I mean. Perhaps the most important exchange is that between the captain and the co-pilot immediately following the bird strike.

For the first time that day, the captain took control of the plane.

"My aircraft," Sully said.

"Your aircraft," said the first officer.[2]

And with those two words, Sully took responsibility for the situation.

He didn't blame.

Or make excuses.

Or complain.

Or stall.

He accepted the challenge even though he never asked for it, realizing this ordeal would define him for the rest of his life. He understood the magnitude of the moment.

His profound explanation to Katie Couric reveals his awareness and carries just as much wisdom as the first time I quoted it in the beginning of this book: "For 42 years, I've been making small, regular deposits in this bank of experience: education and training. And on January 15 the balance was sufficient so that I could make a very large withdrawal."[3]

Sully's poise reflects a certain posture. We also observe this quiet inner confidence in the lives of those who've traveled The Deeper Path.

They accept full responsibility for their lives.

They don't blame.

Or make excuses.

Or complain.

Or stall.

They say to those around them, "My life." And then they step up and live into it.

What defines these people is their ability to focus in spite of the noise produced by the masses talking, economies failing, adrenaline pumping, and life interrupting.

This type of focus arises only when something beyond our immediate pain arises first. Our cross will crush us unless we're able to clearly see our crown that lies beyond. Holocaust survivor Viktor Frankl experienced this reality in a way very few of us will ever understand. Daily his comrades slipped away into the next life. No one would blame them, for they experienced unspeakable pain.

But Frankl transcended his pain. He saw past it and into his potential.

I've broken a few of his quotes down into single thoughts so you can let them seep into your awareness, one idea at a time:

Our greatest freedom is the freedom to choose our attitude.

Forces beyond your control can take away everything you possess except one thing, your freedom to choose how you will respond to the situation.

Life is never made unbearable by circumstances, but only by lack of meaning and purpose.

In some ways suffering ceases to be suffering at the moment it finds a meaning, such as the meaning of a sacrifice.[4]

Frankl understood suffering only makes sense against the backdrop of purpose and meaning.

When we get swallowed up in the moment, we give our power to other people or circumstances. In this space we no longer take responsibility for ourselves, but float along as victims dependent upon the whims of forces outside our control. Hopelessness sets in, the unavoidable byproduct of being subject to circumstances.

But neither Frankl nor Sully saw themselves as powerless. They weren't crushed by their circumstances. Instead, they rose above them and exerted control over the only thing they could: themselves. Captain Sully, only seconds away from almost certain death, reflected on his crown and not the cross that confronted him. He told Couric, "My focus at that point was so intensely on the landing. I thought of nothing else." His commitment and confidence never wavered. "It just took some concentration. I was sure I could do it."

And he did just that.

After he landed the plane and the evacuation ended, Captain Sullenberger wanted confirmation. "After bugging people for hours, I finally got the word that it was official. That the count was 155," he recalled.

All survived.

Couric asked Sullenberger what he felt after he heard the news. He said, "I don't remember saying anything. But I remember feeling the most intense feeling of relief that I ever felt in my life. I felt like the weight of the universe had been lifted off my heart."

Clearly, Sully's crown looked like 155 people safe and sound. He saw his crown and then he lived into it.

Weeks later, the crew and passengers were invited to a reunion. When the crew walked into a hotel ballroom in Charlotte, the survivors and some of their relatives gave them a rousing applause.

"Thank you for saving my life," one woman told Sully.

"You just did an incredible job," a man said. "Really, really, really proud."

"More than one woman came up to me and said, 'Thank you for not making me a widow. Thank you for allowing my three-year-old son to have a father,'" Sullenberger said.[5]

On the day of the reunion, he realized something that few of us ever do.

We're all connected.

All 155 people on that plane are connected to everyone else, even to you. If Sully would have failed to take responsibility for the aircraft that day, then thousands and thousands of people would have been affected.

People would have lost their fathers.

Their future grandchildren.

Their future spouses.

Their brothers.

Their sisters.

Their friends.

Life itself would have been altered, forever.

Or even worse yet, imagine if Captain Sully had crashed the plane in densely populated Manhattan with a full tank of fuel. How many lives would have perished, besides those on the plane?

Thankfully, he didn't crash and so they didn't perish.

Don't think your life is any less significant. You have just as much riding on the way you steer your life—maybe even more. Today, you have the opportunity to land safely or crash. And it all depends on your choice to take responsibility for the gift you've been given.

Your life.

———— ✕✕✕ ————

Reunions. Regardless of the type . . .

Grad School	Military
High School	Family
College	Friends

I haven't met too many people who are neutral about reunions. We usually either love or hate them. Growing up, I always enjoyed our family reunions. I can still remember those annual Sunday afternoons in August at a park in Wisconsin.

The pickup games of football.	The games in the lake.
The scrumptious food.	The competition.
The water balloon fights.	The laughs.
The warm introductions.	The fun.

Reunions blend the past, present, and future into one big experience. The past, because we look backward and reminisce. The present, because we explain our current context. The future, because we anticipate what's next.

In good movies and TV shows, reunions often speak to me. I find myself identifying with the characters. I'm drawn in and I begin to feel with them and for them. Compassion, comfort, regret, peace, hope, fear, love, joy—these feelings emerge at different intervals and in different amounts, based on the place each one of us is at. If we've experienced betrayal, then we process the betrayal of a character differently. It's the same thing with loss, luck, or love. Reunions in media evoke a powerful response, because images and stories speak to our subconscious in a way that information doesn't.

Directors and producers often strategically place reunions at some sort of conclusion. Some memorable reunions are captured in *Les Misérables*, *Tree of Life*, *The Island*, *Inception*, *Gladiator*, *Tangled*, and *Lost*.

Although I can't claim to be an expert about the television show *Lost*, I'll never forget the scene.[6]

In the final episode, a door opens and we encounter Jack dressed in a nice-looking suit as he is led by his father into a very large room. Classical music, with a variety of stringed instruments, fills the air.

He pushes open the door and witnesses many of his friends embracing. We see smiles and relief on their faces. We feel their joy as they reminisce. Each soul reciprocates affection, reunited after a long spell of separation.

We taste their history and understand rather quickly that we, the viewers, are experiencing a rare gathering.

Then the scene changes in a flash, and we observe Jack wounded and wandering through the jungle, looking for a particular spot. With blood-covered hands, disheveled hair, and soiled clothes, he searches intently for something. We feel his desperation, but we're not sure what he's looking for. He feels helpless and lost and so do we.

These two scenes alternate until eventually we get greater clarity about what's taking place. The attendees at the reunion seat themselves in pews, and it's quite clear they're sitting in a church. Jack and Kate sit hand in hand, soaking up this sacred moment.

Jack's father opens large doors at the rear of the church, and immediately a white light shines throughout the entire room. The excitement is palpable. This scene closes with brightness filling every square inch. We the viewers mirror contentment, expectancy, and bliss, just like the characters in the story.

Comparatively, in the other scene, we understand when Jack finds what he's looking for—a certain space on the jungle floor. He falls to the ground and covers his fatal wound with his hands. After a few seconds, a dog joins him and the camera pans out, giving us a view of Jack from above. After a few seconds, we see what Jack sees—a plane low in the sky above him.

As Jack closes his eyes, the screen goes black. The title slide *Lost* appears and then fades. As the credits roll, we see water, land, and an apparent plane crash.

Even when we are only spectators, something about reunions resonates deeply with us humans. If we listen closely enough to the rhythms of life, we'll remember that we were meant for reunion. Life is a journey of *return*—back to the One who created us. Returning to our original purpose. Returning to our full potential.

Stripped down to its most basic description, The Deeper Path is a reunion.

And a happy one at that.

A goal in this life is to live so fully that we enter the next life empty.

Todd Henry, author of *The Accidental Creative*, tells a story about dying empty.

> A GOAL IN THIS LIFE IS TO LIVE SO FULLY THAT WE ENTER THE NEXT LIFE EMPTY.

I was in a meeting in which a South African friend asked, "Do you know what the most valuable land in the world is?" The rest of us were thinking, "Well, probably the diamond mines of Africa, or maybe the oil fields of the middle east?"

"No," our friend replied, "it's the graveyard, because with all of those people are buried unfulfilled dreams, unwritten novels, masterpieces not created, businesses not started, relationships not reconciled. THAT is the most valuable land in the world."

Then a little phrase popped into my head in such a way that it felt almost like a mandate. The phrase was "die empty." While it may sound intimidating, it was actually very freeing because I was suddenly aware that it's not my job to control the path of my career or what impact I may or may not have on the world. My only job—each and every day—is to empty myself, to do my daily work, and to try as much as possible to leave nothing unspoken, uncreated, unwritten.[7]

So what about your life?

Are you pouring out or saving up? Are you waiting or acting? Are you living or dead?

Saint Irenaeus wrote, "The glory of God is a man fully alive." When we're fully alive, we no longer fear death. Feeling peace and not pain, we no longer fear the sting of an unlived life. Instead, we understand that death simply showcases the destiny we've already discovered.

In the movie *Serendipity* the character Dean, played by Jeremy Piven, said, "You know the Greeks didn't write obituaries. They only asked one question after a man died: 'Did he have passion?'"[8]

What about your life? Do you have passion?

When we choose our pain rather than avoid it, we come closer to understanding and embracing our passion. We don't need to *write* our obituary just prior to entering the next life. Instead, we *become* it in this life.

The ancients believed our lives were a story known and read by the world. And if we didn't like the way our story read—as long as we still had breath—we could change our story by changing ourselves.

What about your story? Are you content with the way it reads? If not, why not? You're not too old, too young, too dumb, too smart, too clean, too dirty, too poor, or too rich.

Our greatest work is our own life. And because it's the only thing we can truly control, it's up to each of us to make our greatest contribution. The first step toward changing our story begins by choosing our pain.

Because you're still breathing, you have the gift of time—and that time is now.

The late Steve Jobs wrote:

No one wants to die. Even people who want to go to heaven don't want to die to get there. And yet death is the destination we all share. No one has ever escaped it. And that is as it

should be, because Death is very likely the single best inven-
tion of Life. It is Life's change agent. It clears out the old to
make way for the new.[9]

Don't wait until you die before you choose to live. If you
do, then it's too late. Viktor Frankl gave us perspective when
he said, "The crowning experience of all, for the homecoming
man, is the wonderful feeling that, after all he has suffered,
there is nothing he need fear anymore—except his God."[10]

11

SOUL ON FIRE

Set yourself on fire and people will come for
miles to watch you burn.

—John Wesley

"What's the most powerful weapon on earth?"
Chet asked while sipping his drink at Panera
one Friday morning.

"I don't know, man—and you're killing me with these
questions," I teased.

Chet and I have a good relationship where we can jest.
But sometimes his questions provoke a bit of frustration. He
rarely reveals the answers and seems to find joy in making
others work for it.

"I don't know . . . the atom bomb?" I guessed.

"Nope," Chet replied.

"Come on. Give me the answer," I pleaded. "Is it . . .
love?" I asked.

"Nope."

"Trust me. I'm not going to get this one," I warned.

Maybe he was having an off day, because to my surprise Chet gave me the answer.

"The most powerful weapon on earth is the human soul on fire," he said.

And for the next hour, Chet and I explored the nooks and crannies of that single thought spoken by a French General named Ferdinand Foch.

Fast-forward many years, and I've worked and reworked that quote a thousand times over. Today, I believe that truth so deeply that I've integrated it into everything I do. It's become my motto, my brand, my mission: Igniting Souls.

Even though you might not agree with a soul on fire, you can't ignore one. We observe this quality in the people who have shaped our world the most, people like Martin Luther King Jr., William Wilberforce, Abraham Lincoln, Nelson Mandela, Mother Teresa, Gandhi, and Jesus.

Although there are many more examples in history, every soul on fire knew what they believed and what they valued. They knew who they were and what they loved. They might not have understood exactly how they were going to fulfill their purpose, but that didn't matter. Because they had clearly answered their "why," their "how" was bound to happen sooner or later.

German philosopher Friedrich Nietzsche observed, "He who has a why to live can bear almost any how."[1] Souls on fire know their why, and they ignite everyone and everything they come in contact with. Interacting with them demands a response because they're not lukewarm. This doesn't mean that everyone will accept them. It just means you won't be able to ignore them—no matter how hard you try.

Critics and skeptics will always weigh in with their "why nots." And unless our "why" is bigger than these "why nots," we'll stop before we start. We must decide ahead of time what we want.

A major key to *getting* what we want is *knowing* what we want. Jesus often asked a question along these lines when interacting with people, especially sick people. At times, the all-knowing Son of God seemed cruel when asking the penetrating, sometimes obvious question, "What do you want?" But Jesus never seemed satisfied with shallow conversations. He wanted to dig deeper and get below the surface—as in his interaction with the man who'd been sick for thirty-eight years.

> *Some time later, Jesus went up to Jerusalem for one of the Jewish festivals. Now there is in Jerusalem near the Sheep Gate a pool, which in Aramaic is called Bethesda and which is surrounded by five covered colonnades. Here a great number of disabled people used to lie—the blind, the lame, the paralyzed. One who was there had been an invalid for thirty-eight years.*
>
> *When Jesus saw him lying there and learned that he had been in this condition for a long time, he asked him, "Do you want to get well?"*

What was Jesus thinking? Wasn't it obvious? Of course the lame man wanted to get healed. Why wouldn't he?

A deeper read reveals a deeper issue. Notice the man never answered Jesus's question. He simply told his story. He explained his cross in detail without even considering the crown offered to him at that very moment.

"Sir," the invalid replied, "I have no one to help me into the pool when the water is stirred. While I am trying to get in, someone else goes down ahead of me."

In this particular situation, Jesus didn't even entertain his excuses. He simply cut through the noise and healed him.

Then Jesus said to him, "Get up! Pick up your mat and walk." At once the man was cured; he picked up his mat and walked.

We find Jesus's question buried other places in the Gospels. In the story of Bartimaeus we hear a different song, but the same melody line. Jesus confronted him with the same penetrating question: "What do you want?"

Then they came to Jericho. As Jesus and his disciples, together with a large crowd, were leaving the city, a blind man, Bartimaeus (which means "son of Timaeus"), was sitting by the roadside begging. When he heard that it was Jesus of Nazareth, he began to shout, "Jesus, Son of David, have mercy on me!"

Many rebuked him and told him to be quiet, but he shouted all the more, "Son of David, have mercy on me!"

Jesus stopped and said, "Call him."

So they called to the blind man, "Cheer up! On your feet! He's calling you." Throwing his cloak aside, he jumped to his feet and came to Jesus.

"What do you want me to do for you?" Jesus asked him.

Bartimaeus was different from the lame man sitting at the pool. He's the one who engaged Jesus, and it's clear what he wanted.

But in the other story, it's Jesus who engaged the lame man at the pool. It's unclear what he wanted.

Two stories. Two sick men.

One question. Two answers.

One excuse. One request.

The blind man said, "Rabbi, I want to see."

Bartimaeus knew what he wanted, and he got what he wanted.

"Go," said Jesus, "your faith has healed you." Immediately he received his sight and followed Jesus along the road.

Unfortunately, the lame man didn't know what he wanted. He got something he may or may not have wanted. Plenty of people would rather remain sick and stuck in the familiar than be healed and free in the unfamiliar.

But we're not off the hook. We can't avoid the question, "What do you want?"

Do you want to be healed?

Are you focused more on your cross or your crown?

What's your decision?

Quite simply, some of us struggle to make decisions. Maybe the lame man struggled with Jesus's question too. Maybe he couldn't decide what he truly wanted.

Maybe his indecision has something to do with the very definition of the word. A quick lesson in Latin sheds some light on the subject. The etymology of the English word *decide* comes from the Latin word *decidere*, which means "to cut off," and its cousin, the related Latin word *caedere*, which means "to cut" or "to kill." Our English word *homicide* comes from this same Latin word, *caedere*.

So when we make a decision, we are literally "killing our options." We are cutting off the chance to remain open to other possibilities. In a strange way, whenever we make a decision, we experience a type of loss.

And so many of us avoid making decisions because we think we're preventing ourselves from feeling loss. However, what we fail to realize is that *not* making a decision is actually a decision in and of itself. We'll never be given that exact same opportunity in that exact moment ever again. By choosing not to decide, we are actually choosing to stay exactly where we are.

> *NOT* MAKING A DECISION IS ACTUALLY A DECISION IN AND OF ITSELF.

Dan Ariely, author of *Predictably Irrational*, explains the psychology behind indecision. "Closing a door on an option is experienced as a loss, and people are willing to pay a price to avoid the emotion of a loss."[2]

There is a cost in deciding, but there is also a cost in *not* deciding. These last chapters are completely up to you. It's your decision if you want to continue.

This is probably not a surprise to you, but we're going to go even deeper. We'll move from spectator to participant, from reader to leader. We'll define our own destiny and author our own OPUS.

If you're up for the adventure, then keep reading, but only if you want to become a soul on fire.

12
AUTHOR YOUR OPUS

We are half-hearted creatures, fooling about with drink and sex and ambition when infinite joy is offered us, like an ignorant child who wants to go on making mud pies in a slum because he cannot imagine what is meant by the offer of a holiday at the sea. We are far too easily pleased.

—C. S. Lewis

We had a certain room in our old house with a rather odd name. I'm not sure who named it—probably my wife, Kelly—but eventually our three kids referred to it by this strange name.

We called it the Scary Room.

It's obvious why we gave it this name. The room was inhabited by a few bugs. Anytime we went into the Scary Room and pulled out an item from storage—whether suitcases or toys—we'd inevitably find a stowaway spider or sneaky centipede. Without mentioning any names, certain people in our family were afraid to go into the Scary Room.

I eventually changed the name of the room after receiving an email from my friend Dr. Kevin Doherty, who serves as an emergency room physician. He read one of my blog posts on fear and then he sent me some of his thoughts that originated out of his experience as a medical professional. With his permission, I've included his email below to help inspire some courage within us all.

It is interesting how without fear one could never be courageous. By definition courage is to overcome fear.

It is like the body's immune system. When working properly, it requires an exposure to an antigen before it can develop an antibody. If we never expose ourselves (i.e., The Bubble Boy) we will always have an immature immune system.

Some studies report an infant will develop 12–17 viral upper respiratory infections in the first 12 months. That is normal and they just have to run their course. Try telling that to a parent who is up all night with a child that cannot breathe through their nose, cough, congestion, muscle aches, fever . . . Mom, Dad, child, everybody becomes miserable. It is only normal for a parent to want the magic bullet medicine to make it all go away. Sure, some of these viral infections will develop into secondary bacterial infection due to stagnant mucous/fluid in a nice warm environment (98.6 deg.), like pneumonia, otitis media, sinusitis.

With my older children I think back how many times, out of not wanting them to suffer, I prevented them from the experience of fear, when really I just stole their possibility of overcoming and being courageous. With the clarity of hindsight every well-intending parent could make a list of exposures thwarted by their overprotective fear. In doing so we unintentionally transfer our fear to our child by preventing their ability to develop antibodies. Not only physiologically but spiritually, emotionally, socially, recreationally.

After reading Dr. Doherty's thoughts, I had to change the name of the Scary Room. I didn't realize that I was robbing my children of the ability to become courageous. Plus, I didn't like the fact that our kids were growing up in a house with a Scary Room. Who wants to think back on their childhood with that stigma?

And so I've renamed it the Courage Room. I now see it as a space of opportunity, a space where we can overcome our fears rather than feel conquered by them.

Don't call children's protective services on me too quickly. I'm not planning on throwing the kids into the newly named Courage Room to toughen them up. If they choose to steer clear of the room out of fear, that's up to them. I just don't want to be the one fostering the fear any longer.

Most of us have a Scary Room somewhere in our hearts. There's a door we don't want to open because we're afraid of what we might find. But as long as we avoid that room, then we're not truly free.

While travelling on this Deeper Path, you may want to reconsider that room. Rather than viewing it as the Scary Room, try viewing it as the Courage Room instead. When you're willing to explore that room, it becomes a space for opportunity rather than a space for opposition. I'm inviting you into that Scary Room located within your heart. Once inside, you'll be able to rename it.

Although my Latin skills are a bit lacking, I do know two other Latin words: *labōr* and *opus*. Thanks to my builder, Chet Scott, one of these words (*opus*) has secured a spot on the list of my top ten favorite words of all time.

Here's a peek at each word:

1. Labōr: toil, work

2. Opus: masterpiece, work

Although these words might appear similar on the surface, when we dig deeper we find out they're actually miles apart.

The Deeper Path lead us through our pain, but the OPUS process leads us straight to our potential. And buying into our OPUS means buying into the belief that our lives can and should be our greatest work—our masterpiece.

Once we understand the OPUS process, we have the opportunity to author our own. Authoring my OPUS helped me clarify my purpose. This process took time and effort and, most importantly, a builder who was willing to push me deep.

I'm incredibly indebted to Chet and his transformational work that flows from the company he founded, Built to Lead.[1] Our relationship began in 2001, and he's deeply influenced me. In this chapter I'll share part of the process he created. My hope is that it provides you with greater clarity.

Let's begin by examining a peculiar quotation from a relatively unknown author. He wrote it nearly a hundred years ago, but it is just as relevant today, maybe even more.

> *Masters in the art of living draw no sharp distinction between their work and play, labor and leisure, mind and body, education and recreation. They hardly know which is which. They simply pursue their vision of excellence through whatever they're doing, and leave others to determine whether they're working or playing. To themselves, they always appear to be doing both.*
>
> —L. P. Jacks[2]

I remember the first time I heard this quote. Something inside me jolted free—a part that had been asleep for quite a long time. I thought, *I want that. Whatever it takes, I want that to be my reality.*

The majority of people on planet earth don't experience their work as OPUS—a masterpiece. To them, their work is *labor*—toil. For these people, work is a necessary evil. Such people rationalize their view with clichés like, "That's why they call it *work*, right?"

Not so fast.

Work was never meant to be the problem, but our perspective often is—our disengagement while *doing* it and our attitude while *at* it.

For years now, the Gallup organization conducts an annual study. Although the calendar year changes, the numbers rarely do. Here are the brutal findings:

16 percent of the US working population is actively disengaged.

55 percent of the US working population is not engaged.

29 percent of the US working population is engaged.[3]

Let's look at these first two groups.

16 percent of the US working population is actively disengaged. "Actively disengaged" is a powerful, offensive posture. Remember, it's proactive. This refers to people who are taking action to communicate their disengagement. Think measurable, calculated, strategic attempts to display how they feel. We see their disengagement by their behavior:

Stealing from their department

Sabotaging co-workers

Hijacking meetings

Planting disunity

Spreading lies

These people aren't just in the wrong seat on the bus.[4] They intend to steer the bus *off* the cliff. As a fellow passenger, this makes you a little nervous, doesn't it?

55 percent of the US working population is not engaged at work. "Not engaged" might rank better than "actively disengaged," but it's still not enough. When more than half of a team couldn't care less about their work, then the organizational culture isn't healthy.

At this level, employees' efforts are lacking energy. They do just enough to get by. And when you only "get by," then soon you'll go *bye-bye*. That is, if your boss cares enough to notice. But often he or she isn't engaged either. And when 71 percent of your organization is either actively disengaged or unengaged, odds are that your organization is experiencing *labōr*, not OPUS.

Unengaged employees tell unsatisfied customers, "Hey, don't ask me, I just work here." These players would rather not have their names on their jerseys. They enjoy their anonymity because they're not proud of their company or their role on the team. They're mercenaries, highly or poorly paid laborers who flee at the first sign of trouble.

These numbers are quite similar in other countries around the world. When a person is disengaged at work, he or she is toiling. There's no other way around it. For these people, work ceases to be a labor of love and becomes a job, a burden, and a task to perform.

Disengagement from our jobs comes with a fairly hefty price tag. In the past, conservative estimates have come in between $292 billion and $355 billion a year within the US economy alone.

But there are emotional costs as well.[5]

Swiss psychiatrist Carl Jung said, "The greatest burden a child must bear is the unlived life of the parent."

When disengaged parents or guardians come in from a long day at work and their first response is to "kick the proverbial dog" out of frustration, they're kicking much more than the dog.[5] They're kicking their children's hope and optimism about their own future. Children take cues from what they see. They watch closely and listen intently. If their parents or guardians feel trapped, enslaved, or angry about their jobs, then what hope do they have when considering their own future?

Their undeveloped minds struggle to understand the logic of staying in school only to eventually enter a job they're going to hate. Why exert energy if frustration is all they have to look forward to?

But thankfully, there's another option besides *labōr*.

OPUS. The third group of people fits into this category. Let's discover a little more about this minority.

29 percent of the US working population is engaged. Fewer than three out of ten people are engaged in their jobs. These people take responsibility and ownership of the details. They realize their work is an extension of themselves, and because they're on fire, so is everything they touch.

No one needs to wake up an engaged person. They're living the dream. And don't try taking their dream away from them. You can't, because it's embedded in who they are. As Charles Hedges accurately observed, "A dream is not something that you wake up from, but something that wakes you up."[6]

Engaged people wake up ready to embody their OPUS. They realized long ago that their lives are getting the exact results they're designed to get. If they were ever disengaged in the past, then they stopped complaining and started changing themselves. They found within themselves the ability to choose their attitude and reflect Albert Camus's reality: "In the middle of winter I at last discovered that there was in me an invincible summer."[7]

Tragically, 71 percent of people are spectators within their own lives. They embody passivity and accept their lives rather than lead them. This posture produces stress and frustration. Henry David Thoreau addressed this phenomenon, observing, "The mass of men lead lives of quiet desperation."[8] Oliver Wendell Holmes concluded the lament by reflecting, "Alas for those that never sing, but die with all their music in them."[9]

Misdirected living naturally invites noise because we don't know where we're going. We're addicted to other people's voices because we've forgotten what our own voice sounds like.

The exchange in Lewis Carroll's *Alice's Adventures in Wonderland* between Alice and the Cheshire Cat rings true. Confronted with a fork in the road, Alice asks the Cat which road she should take. In a common paraphrase of the dialogue, the Cat replies, "If you don't know where you are going, any road will get you there."[10]

Truly, life brings forks in the road at every turn, and if we haven't authored our OPUS then each decision is an agonizing, drawn-out experience of mysteriously evaluating the pros and cons. Because we don't have a GPS for our dreams, we roll the dice and hope for the best.

But what is *best*? And how would we even know if we had *best*?

Those of us who have traveled The Deeper Path and authored our OPUS already have a clear picture of what's best. Our thinking has already been done because we know what we want. We've invested the difficult time clarifying what we should say yes to, and so now we know what we should say no to.

Authoring our OPUS is a process that helps us become the driver of our destiny and the captain of our calling.

> AUTHORING OUR OPUS IS A PROCESS THAT HELPS US BECOME THE DRIVER OF OUR DESTINY.

Our OPUS embodies the potential on the other side of our pain, and the crown beyond our cross. We observe it within Bono's melody line, Jesus's passion, Sully's landing, and Gabby's voice.

OPUS, an acrostic developed by Chet Scott of Built to Lead, packs a colossal punch and is a great weapon to ward off disengagement. Understanding the OPUS process opens our eyes, but authoring our OPUS gives us vision. This slight distinction yields huge dividends.

Let's dig into it.

Explaining OPUS

OPUS is simple to understand but rich in application. Here's a quick breakdown:

O = Overarching Vision
P = Purpose
U = Unifying Strategies
S = Scorecard for Significance

Overarching Vision

This is your Big Dream. Remember Martin Luther King Jr.'s "I have a dream" speech? Notice he didn't say, "I have a plan." Rather, he spoke in pictures that lodged deep into the hearts and minds of his listeners. When you write yours (about a paragraph long), don't worry about other people's opinions. Discover your own melody line.

> *Don't ask yourself what the world needs. Ask yourself what makes you come alive, because the world needs people who have come alive.*
>
> —Howard Thurman

> *Dream no small dreams for they have no power to move the hearts of men.*
>
> —Goethe

Purpose

This is the defining statement of your work. Most artists autograph their masterpieces, but expert art critics don't need to read the name of the artist to discover who created it. They know the artist's identity based on the subtle nuances of shade, technique, color choice, style, and medium of the artwork. Likewise, the defining statement of your work should be so distinguishable that people who observe your work are able to attribute it back to you. Your purpose (one sentence) is the way you sign your work.

> *Every job is a self-portrait of the person who did it. Autograph your work with excellence.*
> —Unknown

> *Never give up on something that you can't go a day without thinking about.*
> —Unknown

Unifying Strategies

These are the big buckets of productive actions necessary for you to achieve your Overarching Vision. Most people have too many strategies in theory, but never implement them in reality. Brilliant work is about simplifying. You want 3–5 unifying strategies. These keep you focused and on the right path to make sure you arrive at your Overarching Vision.

> *A designer knows he has achieved perfection not when there is nothing left to add, but when there is nothing left to take away.*
> —Antonie de Saint-Exupery

> *Genius is the ability to reduce the complicated to the simple.*
> —C.W. Ceran

> *The ability to simplify means to eliminate the unnecessary so that the necessary may speak.*
> —Hans Hofmann

Scorecard for Significance

This is how you know you're hitting your target. These are baby steps to your Big Dream. If Unifying Strategies are understood as buckets, then your Scorecard for Significance can be thought of as the content within those buckets. Think metrics, but much deeper than surface topics like revenue or profit. Your scorecard is a compilation of the specific milestones unique to each Unifying Strategy. Aim for identifying three to five milestones for each strategy.

> *Nothing . . . proves a man's ability to lead others, as what he does from day to day to lead himself.*
> —Thomas J. Watson

> *He who looks outside, dreams; who looks inside, awakes.*
> —Carl Jung

> *All human beings are alike in seeking happiness. Where they differ is in the objects from which they seek it and the strength they have to reach the objects they desire.*
> —Os Guinness

A DEEPER DIVE WITH OPUS

At this point, your OPUS might seem a bit fuzzy. Don't worry. Some of the verbiage probably sounds strange because most of us haven't ventured into our Scary Room before. Honestly, very few of us have an accurate handle on our Overarching Vision or Purpose because these aren't topics we explore every day.

Before I share my OPUS or invite you to author yours, it's important to understand what will make your OPUS stick. It's one thing to write your OPUS and hang it on your wall. It's another thing to implement your OPUS into everyday life.

To do so, your OPUS needs a strong CORE. Chet Scott calls it your Six Pack. Just as a strong physical core helps overcome chronic back pain, a strong figurative CORE helps overcome chronic life pain.

Your Six Pack is comprised of these components:

The CORE Six Pack

1. Worldview
2. Identity
3. Principles
4. Passion
5. Purpose
6. Process

Let's unpack these one at a time.

1. Worldview—What I Believe

This is how you see the world. Start each sentence with "I believe" statements.

> *I believe one writes because one has to create a world in which one can live.*
>
> —Anais Nin

2. Identity—Who I Am

This is how you see yourself. Start each sentence with "I am" statements.

> *Until you make peace with who you are, you will never be content with what you have.*
>
> —Doris Mortman

3. Principles—What I Value

This is what defines worth in your life. Start each sentence with "I value" statements.

> *It's not hard to make decisions when you know what your values are.*
>
> —Roy Disney

4. Passion—What I Love
This is who or what you cherish. Start each sentence with "I love" statements.

> *People living deeply have no fear of death.*
>
> —Anais Nin

5. Purpose—Why I Live and Work
This is your "why." Start each sentence with "I help" statements that explain why you live and work.

> *The glory of God is man fully alive.*
>
> —Saint Irenaeus

6. Process—How I Will Do It
This will become your Playbook of Productive Action (or POP). We need our OPUS to POP off the page and into our lives. After you author your OPUS and clarify your Six Pack then you can integrate it with your calendar. Beginning with today, look one month out and organize your next four weeks based around your Unifying Strategies. Each month should contain all of your Unifying Strategies and specific relevant action steps defined in your Scorecard for Significance.[15]

> *Yesterday is ashes; tomorrow wood. Only today does the fire burn brightly.*
>
> —Eskimo proverb

This type of clarity takes time. It can be painful because strengthening our Six Pack doesn't come easy. Developing a physical six pack takes intense effort, and developing a personal one does too.

In the physical sense, introducing acute pain in the form of core muscle exercises (push-ups, sit-ups, planking, and so forth) can help eliminate chronic back pain. By choosing acute pain, we allow our hurts the power to heal us. Likewise, in a holistic sense, introducing acute pain in the form of writing and coaching exercises targeting our CORE can help us overcome chronic life pain. Similarly, by choosing acute pain, we give these hurts the power to heal us.

An Example of OPUS

I'm a visual learner. *Tell me*, and I may understand it—*show me*, and I'm there. In my experience, this is true for many when it comes to the OPUS and Six Pack. I can tell my clients all about it, but until I show them mine, they don't get it—at least not at the same level. For this reason, I included several examples online and in the appendix.

I'll also include mine in this chapter, but first, a disclaimer. This is not my first attempt at my OPUS. I cranked out the first draft in about 2 hours. However, the version you see below has taken me 7 years and counting. The more I revised it, the clearer it became. I've discovered that the more clarity I achieve, the more confidence I have. Welcome to my OPUS.

MY OPUS

KO KARY OBERBRUNNER

Masters in the art of living draw no sharp distinction between their work and play, labor and leisure, mind and body, education and recreation. They hardly know which is which. They simply pursue their vision of excellence through whatever they're doing, and leave others to determine whether they're working or playing. To themselves, they always appear to be doing both.

—L. P. Jacks

OVERARCHING VISION: MY BIG DREAM

Imagine a **tribe** of souls on fire. We *view* and *do* life differently because we know our identity, purpose, and direction—WHO we are, WHY we're here, and WHERE we're going. We believe the glory of God is a person fully alive.

Imagine a **cause** centered on embodying our OPUS and redeeming the day. We show up filled up, experience unhackability, and share our message with the world by serving and storytelling.

Imagine a **space** where clarity attracts. We take ownership, accountability, and responsibility for our lives. Because we prepare for the moment, the moment is prepared for us. We are the most powerful weapon on earth—the human soul on fire.

PURPOSE: THE DEFINING STATEMENT OF MY WORK

Connecting people to a process that ignites their souls.

UNIFYING STRATEGIES: WHAT'S NECESSARY FOR ME TO ACHIEVE THIS?

1. **Personal Growth**: I invest in myself: mind, body, and, spirit. I show up filled up so I can give value to others.

2. **Synergistic Partnerships**: I collaborate with a select few. Together we improve and accomplish more than we ever could have alone.

3. **Transformational Experiences**: I create spaces where people experience deeper levels of self-awareness. These truth-telling events awaken them to what's possible.

4. **Compelling Resources**: I create content. These pathways provide clarity, enabling people to connect in greater ways with their Creator, CORE, and community.

5. **Compounding Influence**: I serve and story-tell. Our impact grows in proportion to the growth of our team and tribe.

SCORECARD FOR SIGNIFICANCE: HOW DO I KNOW I'M SUCCESSFUL?

1. Personal Growth

1.) **Mental:** Because I'm an igniter, I invest time, energy, and resources in the mastery of discovery so I can help others show up filled up.

2.) **Physical:** Because I'm a high performer, I seek uncomfortable, unfamiliar, and unpredictable experiences so I can push myself to new levels.

3.) **Spiritual:** Because I'm a child of God, I think, pray, and journal, so I can worship in spirit and truth.

2. Synergistic Partnerships

1.) **Partner:** I serve select influencers by identifying their needs, providing real solutions, and creating value for their causes.

2.) **Collaborate:** I seek out like-minded leaders and co-create on project-based initiatives that are a business and brand match.

3.) Mentor: I scout for undiscovered creators who need the gift of belief. I provide inspiration and insight to keep them moving toward their dream.

3. Transformational Experiences:

1.) Local: Because proximity is power, I give back to my community by creating events close to home.

2.) Physical: Because our moonshot is global, I go to new places to meet new people in need of igniting.

3.) Digital: Because our world is connected, I guide others into clarity by leveraging technology.

4. Compelling Resources:

1.) Episodes: Because people need to start their day with a spark, I create and publish audio, video, and written content every single day.

2.) Books: Because the written word changes lives, I write, publish, and market books. I leverage these books into sustainable businesses that create passive impact and passive income.

3.) Programs: Because programs solve real problems for real people, I create frameworks and resources that produce visible results in the lives of others.

5. Compounding Influence:

1.) Coaching: I impact the many by coaching the few. These clients reveal themselves by paying the price and doing the work.

2.) Masterminding: I invest in FIRE RING©, a select group of high performers focused on visibly increasing their influence, impact, and income over a concentrated period of time.

3.) Team Building: I assemble, equip, and empower a team of specialists who broadcast belief and ignite souls.

SIX PACK

1. Worldview: What I Believe

- **God**: I believe in the Great I Am—full of grace and truth. God initiates life and desires a relationship with every one of us.

- **Humanity**: I believe Humanity is created by God and in his image and therefore we each possess intrinsic value.

- **Family**: I believe Family is the context where we impart and express our values and worldview.

- **Life:** I believe our Life can be invested in a partnership with the Divine to co-create and bring renewal and restoration to the world.

- **Faith**: I believe our Faith keeps us grounded and centered in an unstable world.

- **Truth**: I believe Truth exists and must be communicated and embodied.

- **Work**: I believe we each have a choice to approach Work as our labor or our OPUS.

- **Abundance**: I believe in Abundance, in giving without receiving.

- **Pain:** I believe potential always exists on the other side of Pain.

- **Influence**: I believe we must earn Influence with others before we try to lead them.

- **Discipline**: I believe excellence requires extreme Discipline, focus, and effort.

- **Time**: I believe Time is a limited commodity and should not be spent or wasted but redeemed.

2. Identity: Who I Am

- **Igniter**: I am a soul on fire put on earth to ignite others.

- **Husband**: I am committed to love and serve Kelly unconditionally, growing closer to her as we grow older together.

- **Father**: I am a father to my three wonderful kids who need to see an example just as much as hear one.

- **Friend**: I am a loyal friend who wants to be remembered as someone who helped them in their times of need.

- **Author**: I am a writer who lets my readers peek into the process of working out my own questions about life, faith, and business.

- **Coach**: I coach a few high performers and help them increase their influence, impact, and income.

- **Speaker:** I am a communicator who connects with people's hearts, souls, and minds.

- **Achiever:** I am a producer who finds deep satisfaction from intentional output.

- **Thinker:** I am a deep thinker who enjoys the finer details of tactical analysis.

- **Strategizer:** I am able to spot relevant patterns and create pathways toward progress.

- **Ideator:** I am fascinated by ideas, and I remember the future through vision casting.

- **Implementer:** I am an action taker who closes the gap between dreaming and doing.

3. Principles: What I Value

- **Specialization:** I value focusing on strengths.

- **Exploration:** I value venturing into new spaces, thoughts, and ideas.

- **Communication:** I value delivering information clearly and effectively.

- **Participation:** I value involving others.

- **Preparation:** I value investing the time and effort needed for excellence.

- **Creation:** I value original and authentic invention.

- **Innovation:** I value intelligent design.

- **Perspiration:** I value working hard.

- **Validation:** I value affirming others for their contributions.

- **Recreation:** I value having fun in what I do.

- **Recommendation:** I value feedback in order to grow and improve.

- **Contemplation:** I value reflection and introspection.

4. Passion: What I Love

- **Ownership**: I love leaving victimhood and taking responsibility for what I can control.

- **Workmanship:** I love making my life my greatest work.

- **Stewardship**: I love maximizing my gifts and talents.

- **Craftsmanship**: I love personal growth.

- **Discipleship**: I love studying and applying Jesus in real time.

- **Followership**: I love learning from others.

- **Leadership**: I love adding value to others and influencing them to become better.

- **Sportsmanship**: I love working with teams and pushing them to reach higher levels.

- **Partnership:** I love aligning myself with like-minded leaders.

- **Showmanship**: I love people who love what they do and aren't afraid to show it.

- **Championship**: I love achieving goals.

- **Marksmanship:** I love accuracy and follow-through.

5. Purpose: Why I Live and Work

- **Recognize:** I help others become more self-aware.

- **Maximize:** I help others create the necessary momentum to start the journey.

- **Minimize:** I help others remove the noise that clutters their lives.

- **Legitimize:** I help others see the value of slowing down and discovering clarity.

- **Organize:** I help others create margin to do life well.

- **Customize:** I help others author their OPUS.

- **Categorize:** I help others identify their signature strengths.

- **Synthesize:** I help others make strategic connections that close their gaps.

- **Prioritize:** I help others do the first things first.

- **Catalyze:** I help propel others forward so they can achieve their dreams.

- **Exercise:** I help others develop a strong CORE.

- **Optimize:** I help others get the best return on their lives by holding them accountable.

6. Process: How I Do It

My POP (Playbook of Productive Action)

- **January:**
- **February:**
- **March:**
- **April:**
- **May:**
- **June:**
- **July:**
- **August:**

- **September:**
- **October:**
- **November:**
- **December:**

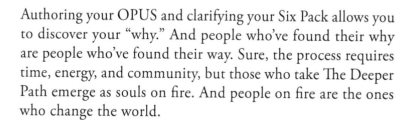

Authoring your OPUS and clarifying your Six Pack allows you to discover your "why." And people who've found their why are people who've found their way. Sure, the process requires time, energy, and community, but those who take The Deeper Path emerge as souls on fire. And people on fire are the ones who change the world.

13

FIVE-MINUTE SKETCH

Courage is fear with wings.

—Audrey Moralez

Just like Captain Sully, we never know when life will call our number and demand a decision from us. We need to be ready for the moment and do the work ahead of time. When we prepare for the moment, the moment is prepared for us. And we are a world in desperate need of prepared people.

Captain Sully daily invested in himself, and life revealed he was the only pilot who could have landed the plane that infamous day. As we add value to ourselves, we make ourselves more valuable.

True masters of their craft realize the power of preparedness and the importance of process. A story about one of the greatest and most influential artists of the twentieth century, Spanish legend Pablo Picasso, adds some color to this truth.

Picasso was sitting at a table outside a Paris cafe. A woman came up to him and asked him to draw a portrait of her on a napkin. He complied, doodling as only he could. After he handed the sketch to her, she was pleased with the likeness and asked how much she owed him. Picasso requested the

French equivalent of five thousand dollars. Aghast, the woman said, "But it only took you five minutes!" Smiling, the artist replied, "No, Madam, it took me my whole life."[1]

Picasso isn't the only artist in the room. Each of us has the opportunity to embody our OPUS every single day of our lives. Our masterpiece isn't some compartmentalized canvas, but rather every square inch of our self.

And one day we will each give an account to The Artist on what we did with what we had.

Every takeoff has a landing.

And every book an ending.

This one is no exception.

Part of my Overarching Vision is watching my coaching clients find their voices and discover their own melody lines. Many years ago, Audrey Moralez shared a few notes from her song with me via email:

> The defining moment is not the glory moment. It is the glorifying moment. It's the gut-check moment. The moment that we decide to look up, show up, and man up. The moment when we decide that God's vision is farther-reaching than our own and we choose to trust His perspective. When fear takes flight and we begin to soar into our potential. Our defining moment is the moment we need to be courageous. And remember, courage is fear with wings.

By now, I'm writing this book with both hands. Funny how pain slows us down in the beginning. This is why so many

> COURAGE IS FEAR WITH WINGS.

people never choose their pain but ignore it instead.

As the weeks wear on, my shoulder is getting stronger, and I'm letting my hurts heal me. Those incisions from the surgeon hurt initially, but they're just scars now, only reminders of the past.

In no time, I'll once again be out on the course playing disc golf and in the living room wrestling with my kids. But to experience this potential, I had to first pursue my pain.

And so, I challenge you to do this thing—afraid. It's been said that if we put an adult brain inside a baby's body, it would take us until age eighty-three before we'd learn how to walk. We'd be so full of fear, self-judgment, blame, self-limiting beliefs, and shame that we'd spend eight decades stuck in an emotional and psychological self-sabotaging cycle.

Remember, stuck stinks! To reach higher ground, we must take The Deeper Path.

Appendix 1
discussion points

These questions, a few for each chapter, are meant to take you even deeper. Feel free to answer them on your own—or better yet, within your community or our Igniting Souls Tribe.

The Deeper Path

1. What are three ways you try to mask your pain?

2. What price would you have to pay if you went deeper into your pain and your potential?

3. Are you willing to pay it? Why or why not?

Chapter 1: A Routine Takeoff

1. Describe one of your "defining moments."

2. Were you prepared for it? Why or why not?

3. Do you feel prepared for your next "defining moment"?

CHAPTER 2: THE MELODY LINE

1. Describe the time when you felt most connected to yourself and to others.

2. In one sentence, describe how you want to be remembered.

3. Are you sitting in the Shire, or are you on the journey, taking the ring? Explain how you know.

CHAPTER 3: LEAVING THE NURSERY

1. How is comfort insulating you from your potential?

2. What are some coping strategies you use to deal with pain?

3. What are some situations in your life that can be defined as "good" pain and "bad" pain?

CHAPTER 4: THE LITTLE DIFFERENCE

1. Which of the seven clichés listed in this chapter have you believed the most?

2. How have those beliefs held you back from your potential?

3. Take some time to identify your cross and your crown. How much clarity do you have?

CHAPTER 5: STEP ONE: QUESTION YOUR CONDITION

1. In what area of your life do you feel stuck?

2. What's your response to being stuck?

3. What's one area of your life where you are consciously competent?

CHAPTER 6: STEP TWO: UNMASK YOUR PAINKILLERS

1. Name a person who believes in you and describe the relevant details.

2. How important is noise in your life?

3. What's the price you have to pay to allow noise in your life?

CHAPTER 7: STEP THREE: EXPLORE YOUR WOUNDS

1. What do you really want out of your life?

2. What are some ways you argue for what you don't want?

3. How do you self-sabotage your potential?

CHAPTER 8: STEP FOUR: OVERCOME YOUR EXCUSES

1. What are your top three self-limiting beliefs?

2. Do you take inventory of why you can't do things?

3. What are some things you can't do but wish you could?

CHAPTER 9: STEP FIVE: EMBODY YOUR HEALING

1. What's one thing you fear changing?

2. What are some specific ways you fear failure?

3. What areas of your life do you fear succeeding in?

CHAPTER 10: ONE HAPPY REUNION

1. What's one area of your life where you've unwisely delegated your responsibility?

2. If you died today, what would you regret not doing?

3. In light of your answer to question 2, is the pain of regret stronger than the pain of risk?

CHAPTER 11: SOUL ON FIRE

1. Is your soul on fire? Why or why not?

2. If anything were possible, what would you ask for?

3. What's a decision you've been avoiding? Why?

CHAPTER 12: AUTHOR YOUR OPUS

1. What's your dream?

2. Does your life reflect labor or OPUS?

3. Reread the quote by L. P. Jacks. In that quote, which word or phrase is most significant to you and why?

CHAPTER 13: FIVE-MINUTE SKETCH

1. What's your biggest takeaway from *The Deeper Path*?

2. Will you visit DeeperPathBook.com and take your next step, whether it's watching the master class, enrolling in the course, or joining our global team?

3. What's the cost if you don't take action?

APPENDIX 2
MORE EXAMPLES OF OPUS

I've included two additional OPUS examples below. Find many more helpful tools at DeeperPathBook.com. Both Linda and Tim were my coaching clients, and both examples are used with permission.

LINDA OUTKA

Masters in the art of living draw no sharp distinction between their work and play, labor and leisure, mind and body, education and recreation. They hardly know which is which. They simply pursue their vision of excellence through whatever they're doing, and leave others to determine whether they're working or playing. To themselves, they always appear to be doing both.

—L. P. Jacks

OVERARCHING VISION: MY BIG DREAM

Imagine a space where people feel it's safe to be real. Where people find common ground and new perspective when they are in conflict with one another. Where people explore new insights in places they feel stuck and discover breakthrough solutions that open doors to their potential.

PURPOSE: THE DEFINING STATEMENT OF MY WORK

Creating space where people feel it's safe to be real and discover breakthrough solutions.

UNIFYING STRATEGIES: WHAT'S NECESSARY FOR ME TO ACHIEVE THIS?

1. **Personal Growth**: By regularly feeding my mind and spirit as well as connecting with mentors on a regular basis, I will give from the overflow of my internal reservoir and increase the value I add to others.

2. **Intentional Marketing**: By being in strategic places on a regular basis to network, by offering complimentary services to individuals and groups, and by implementing other marketing strategies, I will add value to people's lives and cultivate relationships that will lead to coaching and speaking engagements.

3. **Breakthrough Solutions**: Through coaching, speaking, and training, I will create space that allows people the freedom to experience transformation and discover breakthrough solutions. By designing programs that fit my passions and meet needs in others, I will add value to people and work from my strength zone.

SCORECARD FOR SIGNIFICANCE: HOW DO I KNOW I'M SUCCESSFUL?

1. Personal Growth

1.) **Reading:** Read books, articles, and blogs at least fifteen minutes a day.

2.) **Reflection and Prayer**: Pray and reflect at least half an hour each day.

3.) **Coaching**: Receive coaching twice a month.

4.) **Mentoring**: Initiate conversations and relationships with people who can mentor me in both my weaknesses and my areas of strength and for whom I can add value in return.

2. Intentional Marketing

1.) **Public Places**: Make new friends and reconnect with old acquaintances by being available in public places. (Add two names a week to my list of potential clients.)

2.) **Chamber/Music/Church Events**: Attend at least one event each month to add value to others and connect with potential coaching participants.

3.) **Networking Groups**: Become a member of a networking group and attend monthly meetings.

4.) **Complimentary Coaching Sessions**: Contact new people and old acquaintances to offer a complimentary coaching session (one session a week).

5.) **Lunch and Learns**: Offer free "Lunch and Learns" to pastoral groups, community groups, and businesses (one event a month).

6.) **Writing**: Publish articles, blogs, and books.

3. Breakthrough Solutions

1.) **Coaching**: Individual life coaching, business coaching, group coaching, premarital coaching, couples coaching, conflict resolution coaching, EQ-i debriefs/coaching

2.) Speaking: Keynote business addresses, retreats, and conferences for pastors and staff

3.) Training: Team building, conflict resolution training, MBTI team building, FIRO Element B team training, and workshops on corporate values and self-awareness

TIM WALK

Masters in the art of living draw no sharp distinction between their work and play, labor and leisure, mind and body, education and recreation. They hardly know which is which. They simply pursue their vision of excellence through whatever they're doing, and leave others to determine whether they're working or playing. To themselves, they always appear to be doing both.

—L. P. Jacks

OVERARCHING VISION: MY BIG DREAM

To invite people to think differently through various mediums of story. Our interchange of ideas will leave each other with the ability to see the world differently.

To initiate individuals and tribes into a lifelong process of growing, learning, and improving through consulting, coaching, and mentoring.

To introduce resources that facilitate educational experiences and empower people with the love and power of God. These resources will propel people to discover who they are and assist them in unleashing their potential.

To ignite a generation to embrace the will and the Word of the Lord by personally introducing young people to Jesus Christ.

PURPOSE: THE DEFINING STATEMENT OF MY WORK

Propelling people to their next level through the interchange of ideas.

UNIFYING STRATEGIES: WHAT'S NECESSARY FOR ME TO ACHIEVE THIS?

1. **Personal Growth**: Invest in my own growth as a leader through resources, partnerships, and experiences.

2. **Worship**: Insist that the presence of God take precedence in every area of my life.

3. **Concentric Relationships**: Involve myself and add value to others personally, professionally, and spiritually.

SCORECARD FOR SIGNIFICANCE: HOW DO I KNOW I'M SUCCESSFUL?

1. Personal Growth

  1.) **Be Sharp:** Read regularly by reading leadership blogs, the Bible, and a devotional daily, and a book on ministry, spirituality, or leadership monthly.

  2.) **Be Coachable**: Meet monthly with a mentor, someone I have a professional relationship with, where I can communicate my frustrations, share my dreams, and help shape my future. This mentor must be both competent and caring.

  3.) **Be Competent**: Continue my education with Global University, averaging eight credits per quarter.

4.) Be Engaged: Go to two conferences a year, one to inspire me (fill my heart) and another to move my ministry (fill my mind).

2. Worship

1.) Stay Fresh: Take a weekly Sabbath, a day devoted to spending time with those I love: God, family, and friends. The only agenda is fellowship.

2.) Stay Open: Consistently create vents in my life and ministry that will allow the Spirit of God to move freely in any service I lead, any decision I make, and any resource I prepare.

3. Concentric Relationships

1.) Be Available: Meet bimonthly with ministries I believe in. Meet biweekly with people whose destiny I have bought into and help them reach their dreams. Weekly mentor those who want to be in the youth industry.

2.) Be Creative: Interchange ideas through my blog weekly. Innovate products that will add value to youth and youth workers. Inspire students and those who work with students using the power of story. Interact with students from my tribe and provoke them to change.

3.) Be Generous: Introduce myself, my resources, and my prestige to those involved in the youth industry who I can add value to, even though they may not necessarily add value to me.

APPENDIX 3
NOTES

CHAPTER 1: A ROUTINE TAKEOFF

1. Chesley Sullenberger, *Highest Duty* (New York: HarperCollins, 2009).

2. US Airways Flight 1549 Initial Report" (press release), *US Airways*, January 15, 2009.

3. Jeremy Olshan and Ikumulisa Livingston, "Quiet Air Hero is Captain America," *New York Post*, January 17, 2009.

4. Katie Couric, "Capt. Sully Worried About Airline Industry," *CBS News*, June 12, 2009, http://www.cbsnews.com/2100-18563_162-4791429.html, accessed July 22, 2012.

5. The greatest loss of life directly linked to a bird strike was on October 4, 1960, when Eastern Air Lines Flight 375, a Lockheed L-188 Electra flying from Boston, flew through a flock of common starlings during takeoff, damaging all four engines. The plane crashed into Boston harbor shortly thereafter, with sixty-two fatalities out of seventy-two passengers. Subsequently, minimum bird ingestion standards for jet engines were developed by the FAA.

CHAPTER 2: THE MELODY LINE

1. "Melody," *Wikipedia*, http://en.wikipedia.org/wiki/Melody, accessed January 10, 2011.

2. "About One," *One*, http://www.one.org/c/us/about/3782/, accessed January 10, 2011.

3. Jeffery Cohn and Jay Moran, Why Are We Bad at Picking Good Leaders? (San Francisco: Jossey Bass, 2011), 97.

4. *Inception*, directed by Christopher Nolan (Warner Bros., 2010), DVD.

5. Blaise Pascal, *Pensées and Other Writings* (Oxford: Oxford University Press, 1995), 10.

6. *The Fellowship of the Ring*, directed by Peter Jackson (2001; New Line Cinema, 2002), DVD.

7. www.BuiltToLead.com.

8. Henry S. Haskins, *Meditations in Wall Street* (New York: William Morrow & Co., 1940).

CHAPTER 3: LEAVING THE NURSERY

1. "Acute vs. Chronic Pain," *Cleveland Clinic*, http://my.cleveland-clinic.org/services/pain_management/hic_acute_vs_chronic_pain.aspx, accessed January 29, 2011.

2. "Shadowlands Script—Dialogue Transcript," *Drew's Script-O-Rama*, http://www.script-o-rama.com/movie_scripts/s/shadowlands-script-transcript-winger-hopkins.html, accessed July 26, 2012.

CHAPTER 4: THE LITTLE DIFFERENCE

1. Sam Parker and Mac Anderson, *212° The Extra Degree*, (Dallas: Word, 2005), 1–2

2. Ibid, 19.

3. Christopher Sign, "Surveillance videos capture image of Giffords being shot from three feet away," January 18, 2011. http://www.abc15.com/dpp/news/region_central_southern_az/tucson/report:-surveillance-videos-capture-images-of-giffords-being-shot-from-three-feet-away#ixzz1kDZUcW6e.

4. "Gabrielle Giffords Shot: Congresswoman Shot In Arizona," *The Huffington Post*, January 8, 2011, http://www.huffingtonpost.com/2011/01/08/gabrielle-giffords-shot-c_n_806211.html.

5. Mark Kelly, *Gabby: A Story of Courage and Hope* (New York: Simon and Schuster, 2011), 1.

6. "Gabby Giffords: Finding Words Through Song," *ABC News*, November 14, 2011, http://abcnews.go.com/Health/w_MindBodyNews/gabby-giffords-finding-voice-music-therapy/story?id=14903987#.Tx6PaZihCFI.

7. Katie Moisse, Bob Woodruff, James Hill, and Lana Zak, "Gabby Giffords: Finding Voice through Music Therapy," http://abcnews.go.com/Health/w_MindBodyNews/gabby-giffords-finding-voice-music-therapy/story?id=14903987, accessed July 26, 2012.

8. Dan Nowicki, "Gabrielle Giffords' political future still unclear," *USA Today*, January 8, 2012, http://www.usatoday.com/news/nation/story/2012-01-08/giffords-political-future/52453566/1.

9. Amy Bingham, "Rep. Gabrielle Giffords to Step Down from Congress," *The Note*, January 22, 2012, http://abcnews.go.com/blogs/politics/2012/01/rep-gabrielle-giffords-to-step-down-from-congress/.

10. Ibid.

11. Ibid.

12. Ibid.

13. "Passion," *Dictionary.com*, http://dictionary.reference.com/browse/passion.

14. "Passion," *Merriam-Webster.com*, http://www.merriam-webster.com/dictionary/passion.

15. Max De Pree, *Leadership Is an Art* (New York: Dell, 1989), 11.

CHAPTER 5: STEP ONE

1. "The Matrix (1999)," *Philosophical Films*, http://www.philfilms. utm.edu/1/matrix.htm, accessed July 26, 2012.

2. "The Matrix," *Wikiquote*, http://en.wikiquote.org/wiki/The_ Matrix, accessed July 26, 2012.

3. "Memorable quotes for The Matrix," *IMDb*, http://www.imdb. com/title/tt0133093/quotes, accessed July 26, 2012.

4. "70 Million Americans Feel Held Back by Their Past," *Barna Group*, November 3, 2011, http://www.barna.org/culture-articles/ 532-70-million-americans- feel-held-back-by-their-past.

5. "Anaïs Nin," *Wikiquote*, http://en.wikiquote.org/wiki/Anaïs_ Nin, accessed July 26, 2012.

6. "Saint Augustine Quotes," *Quotes.net*, http://www.quotes.net/ quote/42932, accessed July 26, 2012.

CHAPTER 6: STEP TWO

1. "The Poetry of Emily Dickinson: Reader's GuideOther Works/ Adaptations," *National Endowment for the Arts*, http://www. neabigread.org/books/dickinson/readers05.php, accessed July 26, 2012.

2. Pascal, *Pensées*.

3. "Talk: Thomas Edison," *Wikiquote*, http://en.wikiquote.org/ wiki/Talk:Thomas_Edison, accessed July 26, 2012.

4. Michka Assayas, *Bono* (London: Penguin, 2006), 253.

CHAPTER 7: STEP THREE

1. "Memorable quotes for The Matrix," *IMDb*, http://www.imdb. com/title/tt0133093/quotes, accessed July 26, 2012.

CHAPTER 8: STEP FOUR

1. Bruce Lowitt, "Bannister stuns world with 4-minute mile," *Saint Petersburg Times Online Sports*, http://www.sptimes.com/

News/121799/news_pf/Sports/Bannister _stuns_world.shtml, accessed July 26, 2012.

2. Ibid.

CHAPTER 9: STEP FIVE

1. "Simon Cowell Net Worth," *Celebrity Net Worth*, http://www.celebritynetworth.com/richest-celebrities/actors/simon-cowell-net-worth/ accessed June 13, 2012.

2. John C. Maxwell, *The Difference Maker* (Nashville: Thomas Nelson, 2006), 138.

3. Eric Hoffer, *Ordeal of Change* (Cutchogue, NY: Buccaneer Books, 1976).

4. "Biography for Anatole France," *IMDb*, http://www.imdb.com/name/nm0289787/bio, accessed July 27, 2012.

5. John C. Maxwell, *The 21 Irrefutable Laws of Leadership* (Nashville: Thomas Nelson, 1997).

6. "Charles DuBois quotes," *Searchquotes.com*, http://www.searchquotes.com/quo tation/The_important_thing_is_this%3A_To_be_able_at_any_moment_to_sacrifice _what_we_are_for_what_we_could_bec/301242/, accessed July 27, 2012.

7. Hoffer, *Ordeal of Change*.

8. Rick Warren, Twitter post, January 8, 2011, 2:32 p.m., https://twitter.com/RickWarren/status/23869616900018176, accessed July 27, 2012.

9. "John Henry Newman Quotes," *BrainyQuote*, http://www.brainyquote.com/quotes/quotes/j/johnhenryn107044.html, accessed July 27, 2012.

10. Theodore Roosevelt, "Citizenship in a Republic," Speech at the Sorbonne, Paris, April 23, 1910, *Theodore Roosevelt Association*, http://www.theodoreroosevelt.org/life/quotes.htm, accessed July 27, 2012.

11. Marianne Williamson, *Return to Love* (New York: Harper Collins, 1992), 190–91.

12. Viktor E. Frankl, *Search Quotes*, http://www.searchquotes.com/quotation/Fear_may_come_true_that_which_one_is_afraid_of./68749/, accessed July 27, 2012.

CHAPTER 10: ONE HAPPY REUNION

1. "Hudson Flight 1549 HD Animation with audio for US Airways Water Landing," YouTube video, 2:08, posted by airboyd on March 2, 2009, http://www.youtube.com/watch?v=jZPvVwvX_Nc, accessed July 27, 2012.

2. Robert Kolker, "'My Aircraft': Why Sully may be the last of his kind," *New York Magazine*, February 1, 2009, http://nymag.com/news/features/53788/.

3. Katie Couric, "Capt. Sully Worried About Airline Industry," CBS News, June 12, 2009, http://www.cbsnews.com/2100-18563_162-4791429.html, accessed July 22, 2012.

4. "Viktor E. Frankl Quotes," Good Reads, http://www.goodreads.com/author/quotes/2782.Viktor_E_Frankl, accessed July 27, 2012.

5. "Flight 1549: An Emotional Reunion," CBS News, July 6, 2009, http://www.cbsnews.com/2100-18560_162-4783594.html, accessed July 27, 2012.

6. "Lost Ending Scene," YouTube video, 4:21, posted by Oilime87 on May 24, 2010, http://www.youtube.com/watch?v=e3D6EG35WP0.

7. Todd Henry, *The Accidental Creative* (New York: Portfolio Hardcover, 2011), 216–17.

8. *Serendipity*, directed by Peter Chelsom (2001; Miramax Films, 2002), DVD.

9. Steve Jobs, "'You've got to find what you love' Jobs says," *Stanford Report*, June 14, 2005, http://news.stanford.edu/news/2005/june15/jobs-061505.html, accessed August 14, 2012.

10. Viktor Frankl, *Man's Search for Meaning* (Boston: Beacon Press, 1959), 93.

CHAPTER 11: SOUL ON FIRE

1. "Friedrich Nietzsche quotes," *Thinkexist.com*, http://thinkexist.com/quotation/he_who_has_why_to_live_can_bear_almost_any/186996.html, accessed July 27, 2012.

2. Dan Ariely, *Predictably Irrational* (New York: HarperCollins, 2008).

CHAPTER 12: AUTHOR YOUR OPUS

1. For more information, visit www.BuiltToLead.com.

2. L. P. Jacks, *Education through Recreation* (New York: Harper & Brothers, 1932), 1.

3. Kenneth A. Tucker, "A Passion for Work," *Gallup Business Journal*, http://gmj.gallup.com/content/379/passion-work.aspx, accessed June 13, 2012.

4. Thanks for this now-universal metaphor go to Jim Collins, *Good to Great* (New York: Harper, 2001).

5. "Gallup Study Indicates Actively Disengaged Workers Cost U.S. Hundreds of Billions Each Year," *Gallup Business Journal*, http://gmj.gallup.com/content/466/gallup-study-indicates-actively-disengaged-workers-cost-us-hundreds.aspx, accessed June 13, 2012.

6. John C. Maxwell, Twitter post, April 18, 2011, 5:00 a.m., https://twitter.com/JohnCMaxwell/status/59949439560851456, accessed July 27, 2012.

7. Albert Camus, http://bornofanatombomb.tumblr.com/post/2156188098/from-return-to-tipasa-1952, accessed July 27, 2012.

8. Henry David Thoreau, *Wikiquote*, http://en.wikiquote.org/wiki/Henry_David_Thoreau, accessed July 27, 2012.

9. Oliver Wendell Holmes, "The Voiceless," *Eldritch Press*, http://www.eldritchpress.org/owh/vless.html, accessed July 27, 2012.

10. Alice in Wonderland Quotes," *Lenny's Alice in Wonderland site*, http://www.alice-in-wonderland.net/books/alice-in-wonderland-quotes.html, accessed July 27, 2012.

CHAPTER 13 FIVE-MINUTE SKETCH

1. Leda Karabela, "No, Madam, It Took Me My Whole Life," *Why Hesitate*, August 7, 2011, http://yhesitate.com/2011/08/07/no-madam-it-took-me-my-whole-life/, accessed July 27, 2012.

ACKNOWLEDGEMENTS

To my family: Kelly, Keegan, Isabel, and Addison. Life wouldn't make sense without you. You keep me ignited.

To my business partner, David Branderhorst, and our current team that's growing every day: Emily Myers, Abigail Young, Nanette O'Neal, Erica McCuen, Tanisha Williams, Gennean Woodall, Daphne Smith, Debra Hayes, Lisa Moser, Niccie Kliegl, Matthew Waite, Chris O'Byrne, and Brenda and Tim Dunagan. Business wouldn't work without you. You keep the tribe and me ablaze.

ABOUT THE AUTHOR

KARY OBERBRUNNER is igniting souls. Through his writing, speaking, and coaching, he helps individuals and organizations clarify who they are, why they're here, and where they should invest their time and energy.

Kary struggled finding his own distinct voice and passion. As a young man, he suffered from severe stuttering, depression, and self-injury. Today a transformed man, Kary equips people to experience unhackability in work and life and share their message with the world. In the past twenty years, he's ignited over one million people with his content. He lives in Ohio with his wife, Kelly, and three children.

ABOUT THE PUBLISHER

Kary Oberbrunner and David Branderhorst created Author Academy Elite in 2014, rather by accident. Their clients kept asking for a program to help them write, publish, and market their books the right way.

After months of resisting, they shared a new publishing paradigm one evening in March on a private call. They had nothing built and knew it would take six months to implement that idea and create a premium experience.

Regardless of the unknowns, twenty-five aspiring authors jumped in immediately, and Author Academy Elite was born. Today Author Academy Elite attracts hundreds of quality authors who share a mutual commitment to create vibrant businesses around their books. Discover more about the model at AuthorAcademyElite.com

ABOUT IGNITING SOULS

**We are a tribe. We view and do life differently.
We believe . . .**

- Clarity attracts. Confusion repels.

- There are two types of people in the world: those who let the world happen to them and those who happen to the world. Although a subtle difference, this makes all the difference.

- The glory of God is a person fully alive.

- We were created to show up filled up.

- The most powerful weapon on earth is the human soul on fire.

- The most damaging thing in the life of a child is the unlived life of a parent.

- Souls on Fire know WHO they are (identity), WHY they're here (purpose), and WHERE they're going (direction).

Your Next Steps with *The Deeper Path*

 TAKE THE FREE ASSESSMENT:
Get your Unique Score

 EXPERIENCE KARY'S FREE MASTER CLASS:
Find Clarity and Discover your Purpose

 DO THE DEEPER PATH COACHING COHORT:
Become a Master in the Art of Living

 JOIN THE DEEPER PATH TEAM:
Become a Certified Coach | Speaker | Trainer

DeeperPathBook.com

You don't get what you want—you get who you are.
And who you are is determined by how you think.

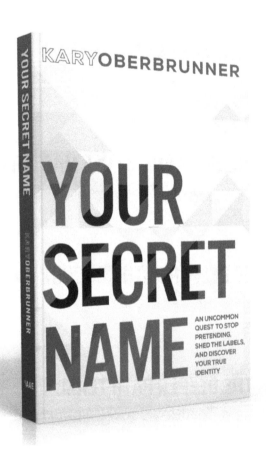

YourSecretName.com

Go as you please, earn as you wish, and live as you like.

Start living your dream job today!

DayJobtoDreamJob.com

Everything can be hacked, even the truth.

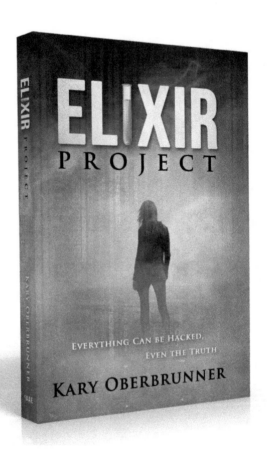

ElixirProjectBook.com

START YOUR DAY WITH A SPARK.

ignitingsouls
DAILY SHOW

WITH KARY OBERBRUNNER

Want to begin your day the right way?
Check out the Igniting Souls Daily Show.
ach brief episode provides practical wisdom for life and business.
et your daily dose of inspiration and start your day with a Spark.

 Listen on
Apple Podcasts

 Listen on Google
Play Music

Watch us on
 **You Tube**

SUBSCRIBE TODAY!

CPSIA information can be obtained
at www.ICGtesting.com
Printed in the USA
FFHW01n1110021018